JCSS Stu

AMERICA, THE GULF AND ISRAEL: CENTCOM (CENTRAL COMMAND) AND EMERGING US REGIONAL SECURITY POLICIES IN THE MIDEAST

Dore Gold

118094221

WESTVIEW PRESS * BOULDER. COLORADO

JCSS Studies
are published for the Jaffee Center
for Strategic Studies
by
The Jerusalem Post
POB 81, Jerusalem 91000, Israel
and
Westview Press
Boulder, Colorado 80301, Frederick A. Praeger, Publisher
ISBN 0-8133-0719-8 (Westview)

Printed in Israel at the Jerusalem Post Press

The Jaffee Center for Strategic Studies (JCSS)

The Center for Strategic Studies was established at Tel-Aviv University at the end of 1977. In 1983 it was named the Jaffee Center for Strategic Studies in honor of Mr. and Mrs. Mel Jaffee. The objective of the Center is to contribute to the expansion of knowledge on strategic subjects and to promote public understanding of and pluralistic thought on matters of national and international security.

The Center relates to the concept of strategy in its broadest meaning, namely, the complex of processes involved in the identification, mobilization and application of resources in peace and war, in order to solidify and strengthen national and international security.

INTERNATIONAL BOARD OF TRUSTEES

Acknowledgments

There are a number of individuals who assisted in making this study possible. I would like to express my gratitude to the entire group of JCSS research associates for frank, constructive criticism during our staff meetings that served to strengthen the thesis of this work. I am particularly appreciative of the Head of JCSS, Major-General (res.) Aharon Yariv, for having originally conceived the need for this study, and for assigning it to me. JCSS Deputy Head and Executive Editor Joseph Alpher contributed his excellent editorial comments and useful insights. Special thanks are in order for Colonel Marshall Michel (USAF) who, as a member of the JCSS staff during 1986-87, willingly devoted considerable time and offered his experience and advice. The sections of this work regarding the regional politics of the Gulf area would have been impossible without the facilities provided by the Moshe Dayan Center for Middle Eastern and African Studies at Tel-Aviv University. I must add a note of intellectual indebtedness to my former advisor at Columbia University's Middle East Institute, Professor J.C. Hurewitz. His rigorous training in the comparative policies of external powers toward the Middle East provided me with the academic background for this work.

ACRONYMS

AOR	— Area of responsibility
AWACS	— Airborne Warning and Control System
CENTCOM	— US Central Command
CENTO	— Central Treaty Organization
CINCNELM	— Commander-in-Chief US Naval Forces Eastern Atlantic and Mediterranean
CONUS	— Continental United States
CRAF	— Civilian Reserve Air Fleet
DOD	— US Department of Defense
EUCOM	— US European Command
GCC	— Gulf Cooperation Council
ISA	— International Security Affairs (Department of Defense)
JCS	— Joint Chiefs of Staff
LANTCOM	— US Atlantic Command
MFO	— Multinational Force and Observers
MIDEASTFOR	— US Middle East Force
MPS	— Maritime Prepositioning Ships
NATO	— North Atlantic Treaty Organization
NSC	— National Security Council
NTPS	— Near-Term Prepositioning Ships
PACOM	— US Pacific Command
RDF	— Rapid Deployment Force
RDJTF	— Rapid Deployment Joint Task Force
REDCOM	— US Readiness Command
SAC	— Strategic Air Command
SPECOMME	— US Specified Command Middle East
STRICOM	— US Strike Command
TVD	— Teatr Voyennykh Deistviy (Soviet Theatre of Military Operations)
UAE	— United Arab Emirates

Table of Contents

Summary

During the 1980s, the US strategic relationship with the Middle East region underwent a fundamental change. For most of the postwar period, the Middle East was practically a military vacuum for American planners. Primary responsibility for the region's defense in the early Cold War was assigned by inter-allied agreement to Great Britain. American attempts to plug the holes of declining British power were constrained because of other American global priorities in NATO-Europe and the Far East. Eventually a US conception arose that assessed the threat of direct Soviet aggression on the Middle East as minimal because of the geography of the region's northern mountain ranges and the deterrent threat of US nuclear superiority. In more highly probable lesser contingencies involving Soviet clients, the United States came to look at its own regional partners — above all, Iran — as responsible for the region's defense. In 1979, with the Soviet invasion of Afghanistan — and with the advent of nuclear parity earlier in the decade — the previous conception of Middle East defense crumbled. The removal of the Shah of Iran exposed American vulnerabilities on even a wider range of lesser scenarios on the conflict spectrum.

With the establishment of the US Central Command (USCENT-COM) in 1983, the Reagan administration converted the Rapid Deployment Joint Task Force (RDJTF), that had been formed in 1980, to a full unified command, thereby placing the Middle East organizationally in American military planning on a par with NATO-Europe — with its US European Command (USEUCOM) — and the Far East, with its US Pacific Command (USPACOM). In 1983 many of the principal features of the CENTCOM area came to resemble those of the European theater: a defined area for regional defense, known as Southwest Asia, emerged; the direct Soviet overland threat preoccupied American planners; all the American armed services were engaged in planning the conventional defense of the Middle East; and US forces were envisioned to have a role at least equal to — if not greater than — local military forces in a wide variety of scenarios. Yet the two zones still differed in important respects: outside of naval forces and military training missions, the US had no comparable peacetime deployments of American forces in the Middle East and — perhaps more significantly — no regional political arrangements emerged, similar to NATO, that would govern their deployment in case of any emergency.

Israel has had little to do with the emergence of CENTCOM. The border separating CENTCOM's area of responsibility from that of EUCOM cuts right through the Middle East, leaving Israel as well as Syria, Lebanon, and Libya under the jurisdiction of EUCOM. Hence US-Israeli strategic cooperation has been focused in the Eastern Mediterranean and not in the Arab East. This limitation, originally established because of local sensitivities, does not take into account many mutual strategic interests that have emerged between Israel and its Arab neighbors. Recent regional trends point toward a convergence of their interests regarding the Iran-Iraq War, precisely at a time when the Arab-Israel interstate conflict has declined as a factor in the regional politics of the Middle East. Establishing a mechanism by which Israel might have a role in the CENTCOM AOR would broaden the parameters of US-Israeli strategic cooperation, entail almost no political costs, and enhance the kinds of regional understandings that could promote the peace process. Just as the NATO alliance has constrained conflicts in Europe — e.g., between Greece and Turkey — these sorts of understandings, albeit without the framework of a formal alliance system, might constrain conflicts in the Middle East in the future.

1. Introduction

Since the end of World War II, US military operations in the Far East — first in Korea and later in Vietnam — appeared to be the focus of American strategic planning and force allocations outside of Western Europe. During the Reagan administration, however, the Middle East has increasingly become an arena of expanded American military presence and activity. This relatively new degree of American military interaction with the region has been apparent not only in Lebanon and Libya, but also and most notably in the Persian Gulf. Strategic concerns with preempting rising Soviet influence in Iran — along with an interest in retrieving American hostages in Lebanon — led the Reagan White House into the complex labyrinth of covert contacts with Tehran that turned into the Iran-Contra affair. Some two years later further strategic concerns with rising Soviet influence in the conservative Gulf states led the administration to undertake the reflagging and protection of the bulk of Kuwait's oil tanker fleet in the Persian Gulf. The reflagging operation, in turn, led to the buildup of one of the greatest overseas concentrations of US naval power since the Vietnam War.

None of these most recent developments in the Gulf region occurred in a vacuum. Prior to the administration's announcement of the reflagging operation (and the accidental Iraqi attack on the USS Stark that thrust the growing American role in the Gulf onto American newspaper headlines), the United States had been steadily expanding its conventional power projection capabilities for the Middle East region generally, and for the Persian Gulf zone in particular. This change was evident not only in terms of the equipment procured during the Reagan defense buildup, but especially in organizational changes: on January 1, 1983 the US Department of Defense upgraded its Rapid Deployment Joint Task Force — created in the aftermath of the Carter Doctrine three years earlier — to a full unified regional command: the US Central Command (USCENTCOM). Prior to this time, the US had established overseas unified regional commands — in which all three of its armed services were represented — only for Europe (EUCOM), the Far East (PACOM), South America (SOUTHCOM), and the Caribbean and Atlantic (LANTCOM). The Middle East, for purposes of planning, was essentially part of the southern flank of the older well-established European Command. With the creation of CENTCOM, the Middle East region in the 1980s seemed to have become a new strategic focal point in its own right.

This study seeks as its first purpose to evaluate whether the military preparations made by the United States over the years in the aftermath of CENTCOM's establishment, represent the kind of change in America's military relationship with the Middle East that is implied by the organizational developments outlined above. In other words, did the establishment of CENTCOM represent a turning point in the level of US military interaction with the Middle East? Is in fact a new pattern emerging — one that was not evident in the previous post-war decades? Historical turning points usually take decades to discern. Nonetheless an attempt is made here to identify such a development, by looking analytically at specific criteria of change. Thus in this study the level and pattern of US military interaction with the Middle East is viewed to be a function of several interrelated variables in every period. These variables may be defined with reference to the following questions:

1. What area within the Middle East is the focal point of American military planning (e.g., Suez Canal, Northern Tier states, Persian Gulf)?

2. What threat is *principally* planned for in the region by American planners (e.g., "brushfire" wars against Soviet client states, counterinsurgency campaigns against pro-Soviet rebel forces, or stopping a direct Soviet overland attack)? How do non-Soviet supported threats — like that of Hashemite Jordan to Saudi Arabia in the 1950s, or Islamic Iran to Kuwait in the 1980s — fit into American planning?

3. What kind of "force-mix" is planned by the US to meet the threats to its interests in terms of
   a. US Army, Navy-Marine, Air Force contributions;
   b. US nuclear and conventional forces; and
   c. overall US and allied Middle Eastern contributions?

4. What is the relative strategic importance of the Middle East compared with other regions of vital concern to US security?

These variables are somewhat inter-related. For example, by focusing on strategic threats contiguous to major bodies of water, the US Navy becomes logically a more appropriate means of

4

projecting US power in the Middle East; conversely, inland threats limit the Navy's utility. Similarly, the intensity of the anticipated conflict is logically connected to the force-mix in any period. At times, however, the force-mix may be a function of independent changes in overall US containment strategy (e.g., New Look or Nixon Doctrine) and not directly related to a specific threat or other Middle Eastern developments. Historically, the designation of a region as "vital" has implied the involvement of US ground forces; but competing security threats in the Far East (Korea, Vietnam) and Europe frequently prevented the selection of US Army divisions for Middle East scenarios. The "vital" designation may not only affect the force-mix; it may also decide whether any US forces are to be used at all. During the Reagan years the establishment of a region or country as a "vital interest" was the first criterion of Secretary of Defense Caspar Weinberger's "six tests" or prerequisites for the use of military force. By using these variables it is hoped that clear patterns of a US military interaction with the Middle East can be identified that will permit some judgment about the extent to which the creation of CENTCOM represents something new.

Unfortunately, little investigative work has been done on past patterns of American military interaction with the Middle East, to serve as a basis for comparison with the current CENTCOM effort. The community of US Middle East area studies experts has tended to show little interest in the strategic-military dimension of American involvement in the Middle East. While the security community in the US has produced a number of excellent monographs on RDF/CENTCOM in recent years, their focus has been primarily Washington-oriented: they are concerned with how their different interpretations of the threat to American interests in the Middle East ought to affect the proportional role of the different armed services in CENTCOM, and hence their respective shares of the Department of Defense budget. This study opens in Part I with a review of previous patterns of American military interaction with the Middle East in order to determine how the RDF/CENTCOM effort of the 1980s differs from past well-known efforts by the US to become involved in the security of the Middle East: the Middle East Command proposals of the early 1950s, the Eisenhower Doctrine, and the Central Treaty Organization (CENTO).

Ultimately, it is hoped to study the implications of these military developments for the current emerging regional security arrangements. If, for example, the United States is shown as shifting from a primary concern with limited 'brushfire" contingencies involving Soviet client states, where US naval, tactical air, or amphibious support forces are most relevant, to a concern with direct Soviet overland invasion — where, under conditions of nuclear parity US ground forces might become necessary — then the pattern of US military interaction with the Middle East starts to approximate the pattern found in the case of Western Europe. Is a new western security structure in fact emerging in the region to facilitate these changing strategic requirements?

The answer to this last question will require analysis of local Middle Eastern forms of cooperation with CENTCOM focusing on the receptivity of Middle Eastern states to different CENTCOM strategies. In Part II, these regional perceptions are fully explored. In the 1950s, US attempts to create different regional alliance schemes did not succeed in most cases because of the large gap between American and particularly Arab threat perceptions. Does this fundamental gap in threat perceptions continue to this day? In the Persian Gulf, the defense of which serves as CENTCOM's raison d'etre, an Arab regional organization has arisen. Known as the Gulf Cooperation Council (GCC), it views regional security as its members' responsibility. Does the GCC see a role for US forces in the defense of the Persian Gulf? Are there specific scenarios which are viewed as chiefly the GCC's responsibility, and others that the United States is expected to handle? Are regional sensitivities to CENTCOM's activities ameliorated by the use of Arab proxy forces such as those of the Kingdom of Jordan?

A third purpose of this study is to evaluate the implications of the creation of CENTCOM for US-Israel relations. As a matter of fact, Israel is not within CENTCOM's geographic area of responsibility (AOR). CENTCOM's western border was drawn to include Egypt, Jordan, Iraq and the Arabian Peninsula, leaving Syria, Lebanon, and Israel in EUCOM's AOR. Several sets of issues are raised by the CENTCOM/EUCOM border. First, what ought to be Israel's role in American security planning for the Middle East region? Since the days of Secretary of State John Foster Dulles this issue has constituted a central strategic dilemma for US policy in the Middle East. The American commitment to Israel has been seen frequently as undermining American efforts at establishing an effective pro-western security structure for the containment of

Soviet power and influence in the region. Israel's exclusion from CENTCOM would indicate that this perception is still the conventional wisdom of the day.

While specific discussion of operational use of Israeli facilities for Middle Eastern scenarios is not appropriate for this type of study, a more general treatment of the costs and benefits of Israeli participation in American Middle Eastern planning is provided. Israel's role in impairing or bolstering American defense efforts in the Middle East must be seen in terms of the kinds of missions CENTCOM is intended for. Possibly, CENTCOM's anti-Soviet mission is difficult to sell to local states in the Middle East regardless of whether Israel is assigned to CENTCOM or EUCOM. Ironically, in its geostrategic impact on the Middle East balance of power Israel may in fact serve as a tacit ally of several pro-western Arab regimes against regional threats of more immediate concern to them.

A second set of issues raised by the location of the CENTCOM/EUCOM border relates more directly to Israeli security interests: Does the emergence of an American-sponsored regional security system in the Middle East — that specifically excludes Israel — pose any special difficulties for Israeli national interests? Here the most basic question to be investigated is whether it makes any difference for Israel if it is situated in the EUCOM or CENTCOM AOR. A second concern from the Israeli standpoint is how CENTCOM activities interrelate with the Arab-Israeli peace process. Is CENTCOM a positive, negative, or neutral factor? By deepening American-Arab ties, is it helping forge the basis of a trilateral peace or is it increasing inter-Arab coordination capabilities in a future anti-Israel war coalition?

The final part of this study draws on the analysis of the previous chapters and proposes a model for American regional security planning for the 1990s. This takes into account the strategic requirements of the US, the regional perceptions of local states, and the requirements of Israeli security and Arab-Israeli peace. Only by addressing all of these factors can a coherent American policy emerge.

2. Past Patterns of US Military Interaction with the Middle East

It might be reasonable to assume that American defense efforts in the Middle East, beginning with the Carter Doctrine and leading up to the establishment of CENTCOM, represent nothing particularly new in terms of the magnitude of American military interaction with the region. Looking back to the first days of the Cold War, the Middle East was in fact one of the earliest points of superpower rivalry. At least two major presidential policies — the Truman and Eisenhower doctrines — were enunciated in connection with the security of important segments of the Middle East. Throughout the 1950s, various well-known attempts were made to integrate the Middle East into the West's global alliance system between the North Atlantic Treaty Organization (NATO) and the South East Asia Treaty Organization (SEATO): the Middle East Command, the Middle East Defense Organization, the Baghdad Pact, and the Central Treaty Organization (CENTO). In retrospect, this period of American self assurance and Cold War consensus appears, if anything, to have been a high point for American global power. This impression of an omnipotent America prior to the Vietnam War and the Energy Crises of the 1970s was best encapsulated by Raymond Aron, who called this early postwar period — when the US erected its containment system around the periphery of the Soviet bloc — the era of *Pax Americana.*[1]

A more careful review of American treaty obligations, however, reveals that the Middle East region was never quite incorporated into the network of American overseas commitments as were other regions of the world. With the exception of Turkey — after its inclusion in NATO in 1952 — the US to this day has no treaties of alliance with any Middle Eastern country. In contrast, US security relationships in other regions are backed by *full treaty* commitments: in Europe by the North Atlantic Treaty (1949), in Latin America by the Rio Pact (1947), and in the Far East both by bilateral treaties with Japan (1960), the Philippines (1951) and South Korea (1953) and by multilateral arrangements with Australia (1951) and Thailand (1954). The US did develop "special relationships" with Israel and Saudi Arabia, but this term represents a political judgment about policies toward those countries rather than firm obligations in international law. The closest commitment to an alliance were executive agreements committing the US to the defense of Turkey, Iran, and Pakistan in 1959; they derived additional authority from the congressionally-approved Eisenhower Doctrine.

Neither the special relationships nor the executive agreements specify the response the United States is expected to make in case of armed attack; neither of these sets of arrangements assures the nearly automatic American actions that are expected in case of a Soviet attack against NATO. No elaborate theory of "extended deterrence" exists in the Middle Eastern theater. Certainly the absence of "tripwire" ground forces reduces the credibility of a firm American response to Soviet-sponsored provocation as in Europe or in the Korean Peninsula.

Of course an analysis of treaty commitments is only one dimension of US military interaction with any given region; American interests and principles may become equally important factors in deciding on the use of force in the defense of a friendly country.[2] This chapter seeks to establish how the Middle East fit into past American strategic plans. Did the region come under an American strategic umbrella — as might be anticipated by the succession of doctrines and regional security schemes put forward particularly in the 1950s? Or did the area more closely resemble a military vacuum, as attested to by the lack of formal American treaty commitments? The thesis advanced here holds that prior to the Carter Doctrine and the eventual emergence of RDF/CENTCOM, the latter description more accurately reflected the US strategic-military relationship with the Middle East region.

As will be seen in the following analysis, the Middle East was relatively a strategic vacuum for the US military establishment due to the prolonged impact of World War II Anglo-American strategic planning on US postwar plans. During secret contingency discussions held even prior to Pearl Harbor, US and British chiefs of staff divided the world into areas of military responsibility according to which the US was to serve as the senior military partner in the Pacific while allied command was to be shared in the Atlantic. In between these two areas — in the Mediterranean, the Middle East, and the Indian Ocean — primary strategic responsibility was handed to Great Britain.[3] This basic division of responsibilities was reconfirmed in 1947 as the Soviet bloc replaced the Axis powers as the primary threat to the West.[4] The US attempted to maintain this essential division of labor by promoting British military leadership over the entire Middle East until 1956 — and in smaller pockets of the region, like the Persian Gulf, until 1971. With this World War II inheritance influencing Anglo-American planning, the US took on its primary strategic responsibilities in Europe and the Far East and committed the bulk of its military resources to those missions.

When the US did become militarily involved with the Middle East in this early period, this generally reflected a sudden recognition that the British could no longer support their assigned role. In fact the entire postwar history of American strategic interaction with the region can be seen as an attempt — under circumstances of limited military resources — to cope with successive British retreats from Greece and Turkey (1947), Egypt and the Arab East (1957), and the Persian Gulf (1971). When the American response to each of these withdrawals is examined from the perspective of the US Joint Chiefs of Staff (JCS), the picture that emerges is of an overcommitted American military establishment advising that it was not prepared to assume the kinds of responsibilities for the Middle East that the White House and State Department were declaring the US ready to back up.

The relative difference between US strategic planning for the Middle East in the past, and planning under current RDF/CENTCOM arrangements, is reflected not only in these revealing attitudes, however. In addition, we may identify several key variables that measure the magnitude of US strategic involvement in the area: (a) the subregional focus of US strategic plans; (b) the identity of the principal threat planned for; (c) the forces designated to meet the principal threat; and (d) the resulting comparative importance of the Middle East as against other regions. These findings are summarized and compared in Table 1.

The Truman Doctrine — The Injection of US Naval Power

The March 1947 Truman Doctrine is usually thought of as an historic turning point marking the beginning of the Cold War and of American efforts to contain the expansion of Soviet influence in Europe. However, geographically and organizationally the objects of the $400 million Truman Doctrine program were viewed as Middle Eastern states: Greece and Turkey.[5] Later Iran was added as a recipient of the new aid program. The threats facing each of these states varied from country to country. Greece, with no common border with the USSR, was in a state of civil war; the principal anti-governmental guerrilla forces received their training and supplies in neighboring Soviet satellites: Albania, Bulgaria, and Yugoslavia. Turkey, which faced no pressing problems of internal cohesion, was subject to potential direct Soviet military pressures. Iran faced both internal and external threats: autonomous pro-Soviet Kurdish and Azerbaijani republics were declared in early 1946, while the Soviet military occupation of northern parts of Iran not only continued after World War II but was even reinforced substantially.

Table 1

Past Patterns of US Military Interaction with the Middle East

	Subregional Focus of US Strategic Plans	Principal Threat	Force Mix	Comparative Importance of the Middle East
Truman Doctrine 1947-	Greece & Turkey	Soviet-supported subversion	US naval peace-time presence	Vital
Middle East Command 1951-	Suez Canal Zone	Direct Soviet overland threat	Primary British responsibility; no US forces	Critical (but third in US strategic priorities)
Baghdad Pact (CENTO) 1954/55-	Northern Tier	Direct Soviet overland threat	Primary British responsibility; US Naval & Air Force peacetime presence; USAF wartime support	Unclear
Eisenhower Doctrine 1957-	Arab states & Israel (excluding Arabian Peninsula); Northern Tier	Soviet-supported subversion	Primary US responsibility; US Naval & Marine Forces; USAF-Army team in USSTRICOM	Vital
Nixon Doctrine (Twin Pillar policy) 1969-	The Persian Gulf	Soviet-supported subversion	Primary American surrogate responsibility	Unclear
RDF/CENTCOM 1980/83-	Southwest Asia	Direct Soviet overland threat	Primary US responsibility; all four services	Vital

Did the United States plan the use of any specific American or allied forces to back up the defense of Greece, Turkey, and Iran beyond a foreign aid program? The Truman Doctrine specifically stated that it was US policy "to support free peoples who are resisting attempted subjugation by armed minorities or by outside pressures.[6] What did "support" mean? Truman stated "our help should be primarily through economic and financial aid...." In early 1948, Secretary of Defense James Forrestal sounded out the JCS about the possibility of dispatching US forces to Greece. Studies already initiated in 1947 indicated that the United States did not have the capability of deploying enough armed forces to Greece to defeat a combined attack by Yugoslavia, Albania, and Bulgaria without initiating a general mobilization. These studies concluded that only symbolic forces should be sent to stiffen the morale of the Greeks. Despite these warnings, the newly formed National Security Council (NSC) staff preferred as a matter of policy to conclude in February 1948 that the US was ready to use its "political, economic and if necessary military power...to prevent Greece from falling under the domination of the USSR." No JCS or Defense Department limitations were placed by the NSC on the use of American forces.[7]

In 1947-48, the only significant changes in US force deployments in the Middle East that seemed to have any relationship to the Truman Doctrine were those of the US Navy. Since April 1946, when the USS Missouri visited Istanbul in order to give the Turks a first indication of American military backing against Soviet pressures, a US naval presence in the Mediterranean had become regularized. A formal Mediterranean task force was established in October; by the end of the year it came to include one aircraft carrier, three cruisers, and eight destroyers. By 1948, this task force formally became the Sixth Task Force, and a short time later, the US Sixth Fleet. A small symbolic naval presence consisting of a flagship and two destroyers, called MIDEASTFOR, was deployed in the Persian Gulf in January 1949.[8]

While these deployments may have given the Greek, Turkish, and Iranian governments some encouragement, it was not expected that naval forces alone would deter Soviet thrusts into the Middle East. American planners, at the time, believed that the USSR would not initiate a general war as long as the United States maintained a nuclear monopoly and upheld its superiority in strategic air power. The American concept of deterrence in the immediate postwar years focused on the value of the atomic bomb rather than on an assessment of the total forces-in-being or the overall military balance. In this sense, deterrence of Soviet power in the Middle East at the outset of the postwar period was essentially nuclear, backed up by symbolic force deployments. These were, however, American assumptions. They were not part of any explicit guarantees to any Middle Eastern state — at least until the later incorporation of Greece and Turkey into NATO. Nor were these assumptions reflected in any force deployments in the Middle East area.

After the 1947 Anglo-American "Pentagon Talks" reestablished British primary strategic responsibility for the Arab area of the Middle East, the defense of most of the region was expected, as in World War II, to involve minimal US combat forces. For example, in May 1948 the NSC requested that the JSC advise on whether the US military planned to hold the Eastern Mediterranean and the Middle East in the event of global war. Short-range emergency plans (HALFMOON) called for securing only the Cairo-Suez-Khartoum area. A marine-reinforced battalion despatched from the Mediterranean to the Bahrain area was to help evacuate US nationals and assist in possible neutralization of oil installations.[9] In fact, despite the growing importance of Middle East oil in this period, especially as a source of fuel for the European Recovery Program, the US in subsequent years continued to plan on the evacuation and demolition of Middle East oil installations in the event of global war. The defense of western-controlled oil supplies in the area, while considered desirable, was simply not regarded by the US military as a feasible mission.

At the time of the Truman Doctrine, the Middle East was held to be of the highest priority to the United States. In November 1947 the NSC determined that the "security of the Eastern Mediterranean and of the Middle East is vital to the security of the United States...."[10] But in ensuing years the focal point of containment shifted to Western Europe (1948 — Marshall Plan) and then to the Far East (1950 — Korean War). Priorities changed accordingly.

Middle East Command/Middle East Defense Organization — Joint Staff Planning

The subregional focus of the October 1951 Middle East Command proposal was the defense of the Suez Canal Zone. The Middle

East Command was not conceived of as a political alliance as in the case of NATO. The concept was put forward initially as a proposal to Egypt; it was hoped that by converting the controversial British military presence into an allied (including Egyptian) enterprise, Cairo's acquiescence would be obtained to continued western allied control of the British base complex on Egyptian soil. From Washington's perspective, the Middle East Command was part of an effort to lend its name to an effort to bolster Britain's continuing strategic responsibility for the region. In fact, earlier, in March 1951, the National Security Council had reestablished in NSC 47/5 that "because of United States commitments in other areas it is the United States' interest that the United Kingdom have primary responsibility for Israel and the Arab states."[11] As will be seen below, American military plans at the time called for almost no American military contributions for the defense of the Middle East. This remained true in 1952 when the Middle East Command was repackaged as a less ambitious training and joint staff planning organization called the Middle East Defense Organization (MEDO).

The focus on the defense of the Canal Zone during the Middle East Command proposals was as much a result of explicit strategic planning as it was a function of Britain's political problems with the Egyptians. With primary strategic responsibility for the Middle East, the British argued that given the West's limited resources the only line that could hopefully be defended in the region had to be drawn just north of Lebanon and east of Jordan and Israel (see Map #1). This line came to be referred to by the planners as the "Inner Ring" of Middle Eastern defense. Essentially, it offered protection to the Suez Canal Zone. American planners attempted to persuade the British to draw a more eastern line for Middle Eastern defense that would protect Turkey and the oil-producing states of the Persian Gulf. This would be known as the "Outer Ring." But American aspirations went beyond British capabilities. The Inner Ring concept thus dominated Anglo-American planning until 1954, when the United States began to stress the defense of the Northern Tier States.[12]

During this period of Middle East defense proposals, the principal threat planned for was a direct Soviet ground attack:

> Although the Soviet Union by this time was an "atomic power," defense of the Middle East was thought of in the West largely in the "conventional" terms of the recent war.

14

Map 1. INNER AND OUTER DEFENSE RINGS IN MIDDLE EAST DEFENSE — 1951/2

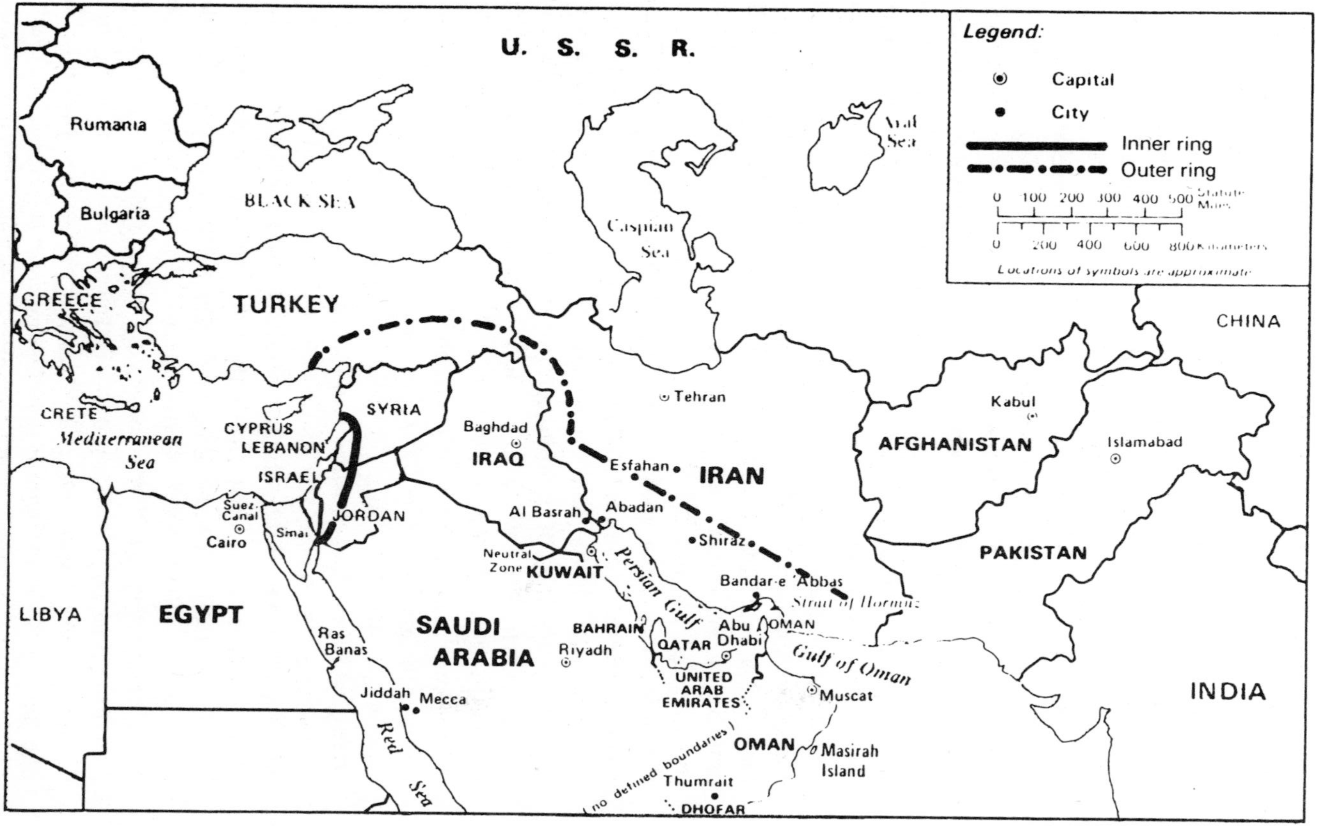

The problem was one of planning a strategy by which an
invading Soviet land army might be checked and thrown
back....[13]

This conception of the Soviet military challenge to the Middle East
was largely consistent with the way new trends in US strategy
defined the Soviet threat, at least according to the basic US
national security planning document of 1950: NSC-68. In order to
handle the threat of general war with the USSR, especially after the
first Soviet atomic test in 1949, NSC-68 recommended the expansion of America's conventional military capability.[14] Planning the
defense of the Middle East at this time in conventional terms was
therefore understandable. In November 1952 the Chairman of the
JCS, General Omar Bradley, prepared a briefing for the Department of Defense which more specifically defined the principal
threat considered at the time for allied force planning. The USSR
was assessed to have the capability of building up its ground
forces against Turkey and Iran to 13 1/3 divisions within five
months of the outbreak of a general war, with a potential of
reaching 20 1/3 divisions within seven months. Soviet combat
airpower — estimated at 1400 aircraft in this theater — was
chiefly tactical; it was viewed essentially as providing air support
to the ground campaign or, alternatively, as a means of interrupt-
ing allied sea lines of communication in the Mediterranean from
advanced bases seized by the ground forces. Soviet naval capabilities at this time were minimal.[15]

The American military establishment continually resisted any
attempt in this period to give American combat units responsibilities in the Middle East. US global war plans in 1952 did not
contemplate the use of American forces in the region. Against the
Soviet ground threat, the chairman of the JCS expected that a
combined western force of 12 divisions could be raised consisting
of 10 Turkish divisions, one British division, and one division
combining Jordanian and Iraqi elements. All combat aircraft were
expected to come from the British. It was hoped that over the next
three years western forces might be expanded to 18 divisions,
including possible new contributions from Iran and Israel; no new
US force contributions were foreseen either in the ground or air
campaigns. General Omar Bradley viewed US participation in
Middle East security in 1952 as largely symbolic: "The US cannot
send troops to the area....The US would be willing to contribute to
the staff of a Middle East defense organization largely as a means

16

of securing the participation of others in such an arrangement."[16]

These limitations on American military involvement in the Middle East were reflected in discussions over the relative importance of the region. During the early part of the 1950s a protracted debate went on among the departments of state and defense as well as among the different armed services over whether the Middle East was "vital" or "critical" for US strategic planning. The Defense Department, for its part, was less anxious than State to supplant the British in the area.[17] As for the armed services, the US Army strongly opposed the American assumption of strategic responsibilities in the Middle East. US Army Chief of Staff General J. Lawton Collins even opposed military missions to Saudi Arabia, Syria, Lebanon and Israel in 1951 lest "the people of the Middle East" think that in the event of war "we will send troops and aircraft." He bluntly stated: "We are kidding ourselves and kidding them if we do anything which indicates that we are going to put forces in that area. The forces to do that are not in sight."[18] Designation of the Middle East as "vital" implied the commitment of ground forces to its defense. The Navy, on the other hand, was assumed to support the "vital" designation, not only because of its growing use of Middle Eastern oil, but also because a ground force role would significantly expand its missions of supply and sea lane defense in the region. In 1951 the National Security Council determined that the region was of "critical importance" to the security of the US.[19]

In the view of the State Department, JCS plans in 1951 implied "that the United States contemplates the abandonment, without even a token defense effort, of most if not all the Middle East in time of global war."[20] The JCS Chairman defended this situation: "we just feel we cannot defend Europe and the Middle East at the same time — we could still win a war despite the loss of the Middle East, which would not be true of Europe."[21] In 1952 American priorities placed the Middle East not only after Europe but after the Far East as well; outlining the conditions of American participation in Middle East defense arrangements, Bradley concluded:

> ...The JCS believe that we should provide what military assistance we can to the countries in the area without upsetting our present priorities.
>
> The JCS does not believe that these priorities should be changed. The priorities now are (a) Korea, (b) Indochina, (c) The US and NATO.[22]

Baghdad Pact/ CENTO — US Air Support in the Middle East

US military strategy in the Middle East under the Eisenhower administration was a product of two fundamental inputs. First, as a consequence of his famous tour of the Middle East in 1953, Secretary cf State John Foster Dulles concluded that future efforts to set up a regional defense organization must focus on those states most directly threatened by the USSR (and hence most willing to participate). The strategic focus of American planning thus shifted away from the Suez Canal Zone (and Egypt) and returned to the "Northern Tier" countries bordering the USSR.

A second input to US Middle East strategy in this period was the "New Look" defense posture that the administration was implementing in Washington. Determined to achieve a balanced budget, the administration preferred to concentrate on the development of US strategic nuclear airpower rather than pursue the costly expansion of both nuclear and conventional forces. Thus while in the Eisenhower years the Strategic Air Command (SAC) experienced steady growth, the US Army was cut by a third, as were the US Air Force's troop carrier wings.[23] Under these circumstances, the chances that the US might assume greater responsibility for Middle Eastern defense, including the commitment of ground forces, were slight. This certainly served as one of the inhibiting military factors on American adherence to the series of treaties between Turkey, Iraq, Iran, Pakistan, and Great Britain in 1955 that came to be known as the Baghdad Pact. Diplomatic factors included an American desire not to alienate Egypt entirely, as well as the problem of openly allying with Iraq in light of the latter's approach to Israel. The US continued to remain formally outside the Baghdad Pact, even after the pro-western Hashemite monarchy in Iraq was overthrown in July 1958 and the Baghdad Pact Organization, now excluding Iraq, was renamed the Central Treaty Organization (CENTO) a little over a year later.

There was no substantial change in the perception of the primary threat to the Middle East in US strategic planning for the defense of the Northern Tier states. A 15 to 20 division Soviet ground force in the Transcaucasus was seen as being capable of reaching the oil-producing areas of Iran, Kuwait, and Saudi Arabia.[24] Growing Soviet nuclear strength became an increasingly significant factor in considering the vulnerability of western strategies that concentrated allied forces in one easily targetable area (e.g., the Suez Canal Zone).[25] While the basic document on US national security policy in these years, NSC 162/1, did not anticipate that the USSR would deliberately launch a general war by attacking the United States or its allies, it did express concern that "increasing Soviet atomic capability may tend to diminish the deterrent effect of US atomic power against peripheral Soviet aggression."[26] The Middle East, excluding Greece and Turkey, remained outside the US treaty system; the overall global balance of strategic forces could not protect the region unless the United States clarified its commitments to the area.

As already noted, New Look cutbacks in US conventional forces meant US ground forces could not be expected to participate in the defense of the Middle East. However, new possibilities for some expanded US military role arose in connection with the increasing use of the region by the Strategic Air Command as a platform for operations against the USSR. The United States acquired forward air base rights in Morocco (1950) and Libya (1954). Until the introduction of the intercontinental range B-52 at the end of the decade made them obsolete, these bases primarily served American global strategic rather than specifically Middle Eastern interests. Nevertheless, they constituted an additional American military presence in the area and could be considered for use in contingency plans for Middle East defense.

After 1957, as the United States increased its participation in the military committee of the Baghdad Pact — without officially joining the organization — American military plans were already making use of US air assets in the region. The Middle East Emergency Defense Plan (ME-EDP 1-58), developed between late 1957 and early 1958, provided for the employment of US forces normally found in the Middle East. Aside from the small number of personnel attached to US military missions and the American naval presence, the plan specifically referred to the participation of American airpower in the defense of the Middle East. In the words of the official *JCS History,*

> The concept of operations was that the scheduled US strategic air attack against installations and troop concentration points in Soviet areas adjacent to the Middle East would "drastically reduce the Soviet air, ground, and nuclear threat," so that indigenous forces might be able to hold the enemy by their defense.[27]

With the massive British presence removed from Suez — smaller forces were dispersed between Cyprus and Aden — and the loss of Iraqi manpower after the anti-Hashemite coup in Baghdad, the "indigenous forces" expected to hold back the Soviets could only come from Turkey and Iran. Not surprisingly, given these weaknesses in the western ground defense of the Middle East, the United States partially extended its umbrella to the Northern Tier in 1959, when it signed individual executive security agreements with Turkey, Iran, and Pakistan. Washington still refrained from joining the Baghdad Pact or its successor organization CENTO.

From Dulles' 1953 trip to the region to the American landing in Lebanon in 1958, the Middle East was a high priority area for US national security policy. Military aid programs were initiated and expanded in this period. Yet overall military strategy limited the extent to which the United States could fully inject itself into the region even after the British position collapsed in 1956. Besides the possible use of American airpower in general war contingencies, the rapid decline in British strength was forcing the United States to involve itself in another set of security problems that arose from the increasing threat of limited inter-regional war. Thus in tandem with an increasing commitment to the Northern Tier, the Eisenhower administration planned for an entirely different set of limited contingencies in the Israel-Arab zone. This was reflected in the Eisenhower Doctrine.

The Eisenhower Doctrine — Toward a Limited War Strategy

Soviet arms sales to the Arab world began in 1955. They were shortly followed by a surge of pro-Soviet sentiment after the failed Anglo-French assault against Egypt permitted Moscow to leapfrog over the Northern Tier barrier established by the Baghdad Pact and acquire positions of influence in the heart of the Middle East. Out of a concern for Soviet exploitation of the western vacuum in the Arab states, President Eisenhower addressed Congress on January 5, 1957 and called for a joint resolution authorizing economic and military aid as well as the use of US armed forces in support of any Middle Eastern state "faced with overt armed aggression from a country controlled by international communism." With slight modification, the president's request was approved in March and came to be known as the Eisenhower Doctrine.

Like the Truman Doctrine ten years earlier, the Eisenhower Doctrine was invoked in case of externally supported internal threats to Middle Eastern regimes such as that perceived during the Jordan crisis of 1957 and the more famous Lebanon crisis of 1958. Both threats involved subversive operations against pro-western regimes that were attributed to the newly created United Arab Republic. The latter's pro-Soviet alignment presumably placed it in the category of "a country controlled by international communism." In congressional hearings, Dulles specifically excluded from the doctrine's jurisdiction threats of aggression from non-communist sources.[28] Questions as to whether pro-Nasserist groups in Jordan or Lebanon could really be tied to "international communism" or whether they could be deterred by the movements of US forces raised considerable doubt in ensuing years over the wisdom and efficacy of the doctrine.

As for the threat of a direct Soviet attack on the Middle East, Dulles had now concluded that such a contingency did not seem imminent. Moreover, this time it was not clear that such an attack could remain localized; fighting against such an assault, with the administration's heavy stress on strategic nuclear forces, would no longer entail a replay of the conventional battles of World War II. According to JCS Chairman Admiral Arthur W. Radford, an overt Soviet attack in the Middle East would initiate a third world war.[29] Presumably, the administration felt that in light of the threat of "massive retaliation," the USSR no longer had a real direct attack option against the Middle East.

The Eisenhower Doctrine stimulated considerable American military planning for the Middle East. Unlike the early 1950s, much of this planning excluded Great Britain. The latter had clearly become the United States' junior partner in the overall defense of the Middle East; its special position according to presidentially approved policy in NSC 5820/1 was focused in "the Persian Gulf and the Arabian Peninsula."[30] The Joint Chiefs of Staff had not been consulted before the declaration of the Eisenhower Doctrine and only in its aftermath did they begin to consider its military implications. In one of the earliest of these studies they noted that in the event of an "extreme Soviet reaction" to the president's statement "in the form of direct military aggression," the result would be general war for which detailed plans already existed. However, the JCS noted that there was a danger that a Middle Eastern state under Soviet influence might "launch aggressive action against neighboring states;" while it was expected that existing plans might be modified in such a contingency, the JCS admitted "there are no plans especially designed to deal with Communist-inspired limited war in the Middle East."[31]

One significant recommendation made at this early stage by the JCS was the establishment of a multiservice unified command for the Middle East area (MECOM) that would assume responsibility for strategic planning and coordinate military programs with the local states. With both the Navy and the Air Force increasingly involved in the Middle East in the 1950s, this recommendation now added the US Army as an additional armed service with an interest in the security of the region. The US Army was already assuming substantial Middle Eastern responsibilities in 1958 during the Lebanon landing; US Army airborne units from Germany, comprising some 8,515 personnel, outnumbered the more well-known Marine presence that reached only 5,842.[32] The Department of Defense appeared to implement this JCS idea partially in subsequent years when the responsibilities of the Commander-in-Chief of US Naval Forces Eastern Atlantic and Mediterranean (USCINCNELM) were broadened. For much of the 1950s, USCINCNELM was both the naval component commander of the US European Command (USEUCOM) and commander of US Specified Command, Middle East (USSPECOMME). On February 3, 1960, CINCNELM was directed to establish a unified multi-service staff for Middle Eastern planning separate from his exclusively naval staff that dealt with his European responsibilities. This arrangement, it must be added, was regarded as only temporary until MECOM was established.[33]

Ironically, the intervention forces to support the Eisenhower Doctrine were really created by the successor Kennedy administration — whose proposed defense strategy was based on a critique of the containment policies of the 1950s. The Kennedy-McNamara Pentagon was concerned with the state of US conventional forces after years of the New Look buildup of US strategic nuclear power, as well as with the increasing likelihood of Soviet-sponsored limited war threats to the Third World. After proposing a substantial enlargement of the size of US Army forces based in the continental US, the Kennedy administration created in

October 1961 a new unified command, the US Strike Command (US STRICOM), chiefly for operations in "brushfire" wars in the Third World. In December 1963, STRICOM took over unified command responsibility for the Middle East from CINCNELM.[34] STRICOM was a multiservice command in that it combined the army assets of the Strategic Army Corps and the air force assets of the Tactical Air Command in the continental US. It was not assigned any substantial naval or marine units. In the course of the 1960s, STRICOM's ability to become an intervention force for the Middle East diminished as it took responsibility for the mobilization and deployment of most of its assigned forces to Southeast Asia. Again US commitments and priorities regarding other regions handicapped its ability to assume strategic responsibilities for the Middle East.

The Nixon Doctrine / Twin Pillar Policy — Allied Burdensharing in Gray Area Contingencies

The chances of increasing the level of American military interaction with the Middle East under the Nixon administration were severely limited by its overall national security strategy for lesser conflicts in the Third World — known as the Nixon Doctrine. Facing an eventual troop withdrawal from Vietnam through the Vietnamization program, the Nixon-Kissinger team sought a means to clarify to its nervous Asian allies the parameters of its military obligations despite the growing anti-interventionist consensus in Washington. In short, the Nixon Doctrine was thought of as a means for the United States to draw the line on the extent of its military involvement overseas — it would still counter nuclear threats from the Soviets and Chinese — without creating the impression of any abandonment of responsibilities. The Nixon Doctrine, furthermore, was conceived in a specific foreign and defense policy framework. As the United States initiated its opening to China and detente with the USSR, the doctrine was developed in the expectation of a more relaxed East-West relationship. Similarly, US defense policy was calling for a revision of the Kennedy-McNamara "2 1/2 war" strategy — that anticipated meeting simultaneous Soviet and Chinese attacks as well as another lesser contingency — to a new "1 1/2 war" strategy — of countering *either* Soviet or Chinese attacks, as well as another lesser contingency.[35]

The Nixon Doctrine became relevant in the Middle East not so much for redefining earlier obligations — as in Asia — but rather in planning how to handle new ones. With the January 1968 announcement by Britain of its planned withdrawal from the Persian Gulf — the last of its Middle Eastern strongholds — the United States was faced with yet another potential Middle Eastern vacuum. Would it replace Britain in the Gulf as it had attempted in Greece and Turkey with the Truman Doctrine, or in the Israel- Arab zone with the Eisenhower Doctrine? Following the guidelines of the Nixon Doctrine, it did not do so. Rather it chose to look to the two most powerful pro-western states in the Gulf — Iran and Saudi Arabia — as the guarantors or "twin pillars" of regional security. The division of responsibilities between these regional surrogate powers and the United States in "half-war" contingencies is considered below.

Against what theaters were the Nixon Doctrine and the twin pillar policy conceived? As in the Kennedy-McNamara era less emphasis was placed on handling a direct Soviet attack on the Middle East or the Gulf sub-region. According to testimony by the then Deputy Assistant Secretary of Defense (ISA) for Near Eastern, African, and South Asian Affairs, James Noyes,

> with the gradual improvement in relations between the USSR and Iran and between the USSR and ourselves, *the threat of Soviet military action* against the sovereignty and independence of states in the Persian Gulf and the Arabian Peninsula *has lessened and is no longer a cause of immediate concern* [emphasis added].[36]

If the Soviets represented any threat at all to the region, according to Noyes, it arose in connection with their "desire to increase influence, to possibly assist subversion in the areas." Moreover, at least three pro-western regimes faced inter-state threats from countries that received substantial military support from the USSR: Iran and Kuwait were primarily preoccupied with the Iraqi threat, while Saudi Arabia was concerned with both Iraq and the People's Democratic Republic of Yemen (PDRY).

What force-mix was conceived to handle the threats to the Gulf subregion? The Nixon Doctrine attempted to divide US and regional allied responsibilities globally as follows:

1. strategic nuclear warfare — primary reliance to be placed

on US strategic deterrent forces;

2. theater nuclear warfare — has primary responsibility; allied participation according to allied nuclear capabilities;

3. theater conventional warfare — shared US and allied responsibility:

4. subtheater or localized war — the threatened ally bears primary responsibility; US assistance to be provided according to interests or obligations.[37]

These categories were, of course, rough guidelines of policy. The US reaction in every crisis would have to be considered independently. At the highest level of violence, nuclear attack in the Middle East — the United States was expected to assume primary strategic responsibility. But what would happen in a Soviet theater conventional attack on Iran? Was Iran expected to supply the ground forces while the United States furnished air support as in the plans of the late 1950s? One indication of the probable US reaction in such a scenario can perhaps be taken from American behavior at the end of the October 1973 Arab-Israel war. Faced with the threat of the injection of Soviet conventional forces in the Middle East, the United States responded by escalating to a nuclear alert. As will be seen below, US conventional capabilities at this time were not sufficient for almost any other scenario in the Middle East.

Clearly in the Gulf region, given the threats to stability that were considered most likely, the local "pillars" were to have primary responsibility. Certainly they were to handle problems of internal subversion. The classic example of the twin pillar policy at work was the Iranian anti-insurgency operation against the PDRY-supported Dhufar rebellion in Oman. Regarding inter-state threats, like a repetition of the 1961 Iraqi threat against Kuwait, it was hoped that Saudi and/or Iranian forces in conjunction with Kuwaiti forces might stop the Iraqis. US participation under such circumstances could not be ruled out, but certainly would be a function of American force dispositions worldwide.

Under the Nixon Doctrine the exact division of responsibilities between US and regional forces in such inter-state, or, in the words of Henry Kissinger, "gray area" conflicts was not firmly established in any single formula. The role of US forces in these brushfire contingencies could be expected to be minimal. While the US defense posture included the half-war capability referred to above, in practice as long as American military involvement in Vietnam continued, few forces were available for other regional conflicts. Thus Henry Kissinger notes that during the September 1970 Jordan crisis, the United States had only four brigades available for reaching Jordan. Taking one brigade from Germany and the three brigades constituting the 82nd Airborne Division, Kissinger noted, "such an operation would enlist our entire strategic reserve."[38] These force limitations led Kissinger to conclude that in the event of a Syrian or Iraqi move into Jordan, Israel would assume principal responsibility for ground operations while the United States would deter Soviet intervention against Israel. In keeping with this limited US role in regional conflicts under the Nixon Doctrine, the Defense Department disestablished US STRICOM in July 1971, thereby eliminating America's principal overseas interventionist command; US forces in the Middle East subsequently came under the US European Command. STRICOM's training responsibilities were inherited by the newly created US Readiness Command (US REDCOM).[39]

One of the ironies of the Nixon-Kissinger period was that precisely at a time when the strategic importance of the Middle East was increasing due to the energy crisis, US capabilities to assume responsibilities in the region were at a low point. By 1969, with the American withdawal from Wheelus Air Force Base in Libya, the United States had lost the last of its great Middle Eastern air bases. The US still retained important facilities in Turkey, but difficulties in US-Turkish relations in the wake of the 1974 Turkish invasion of Cyprus raised some doubt regarding their accessibility for non-NATO contingencies. The Sixth Fleet still remained the principal ready force for projecting American power in the Middle East, but as the focus of US concern in the region shifted from the Eastern Mediterranean to the Persian Gulf, its limited utility became readily apparent. In the Indian Ocean, the United States had only the small symbolic MIDEASTFOR. Carrier visits to the Arabian Sea became more frequent after 1973, but their regular deployment would have to await the crises in Iran at the end of the decade. The US Navy buildup of its communications facility at Diego Garcia at the center of the Indian Ocean, first secured in 1966, was still in its infancy in the mid-1970s. Its expansion as a real combat support base would also have to wait several years. Finally, cutbacks in the number of active US Army divisions in the mid-1970s meant even fewer extra forces were available for non-NATO/East Asian contingencies, despite the Vietnam withdrawal.

Looking at the postwar pattern of US military interaction with the Middle East up to the emergence of the Rapid Deployment Force in 1980, and its successor CENTCOM, what common features emerge? First, US military involvement in the Middle East was piecemeal, generally corresponding to a succession of British withdrawals from different parts of the region. By the time the British completed the last of their great withdrawals, the United States had already given primary security commitments to other regions. Unlike in Europe or the Far East, no regional security system under US leadership rose in the Middle East. Secondly, while plans for handling direct Soviet threats to the region doubtless existed for most of the period covered, from the time of the Eisenhower Doctrine (1957) onward the United States was increasingly preoccupied with threats of internal subversion and inter-state conflict in the Middle East. For the less likely case of direct Soviet military expansion — whether nuclear or conventional — initially the US relied on its strategic nuclear superiority and later on a more modest favorable strategic nuclear balance. For the more likely cases of subversion or inter-state war, for a brief period under the Eisenhower Doctrine the United States indicated a readiness to inject forces that in any case were readily available near the Middle East in order to support friendly western governments. As the growing commitment in Vietnam made such new responsibilities more difficult to assume, these lesser contingencies became increasingly the responsibilities of regional-surrogate powers as recognized by the Nixon Doctrine.

To the extent to which the United States did make forces available for the complete range of threats to the Middle East in these years, its task was made simpler by the proximity of these threats to strategic systems deployed for the defense of Europe and their availability for Middle Eastern scenarios. The principal armed services involved with the defense of the Middle East for the period under review were the forward deployed units, initially of the US Navy and subsequently of the US Air Force. The US Army, despite the one-time Lebanon landing and attempts to establish the US Strike Command, never assumed the same degree of responsibility for Middle Eastern scenarios as its sister services.

Strategic developments in the 1970s, however, placed new burdens on the navy and the air force, affecting the prospects of their continued involvement in the region. First, the loss of the US Air Force's Middle Eastern bases during the 1960s removed an important platform for US participation in air campaigns over the Middle East. The consequent reliance on NATO European bases and on European permission to use them for non-NATO contingencies, complicated American plans for the area. Secondly, as the center of American strategic concern shifted from the Eastern Mediterranean to the Persian Gulf area, US naval participation in Middle Eastern defense was complicated as well. The Sixth Fleet, deployed to serve the southern flank of NATO, could no longer be assumed to cover US interests in the Middle East as well, especially as they became distanced beyond the range of its carrier aircraft and marine amphibious forces. In the Indian Ocean, the United States had no regularly deployed forces to pick up where the Sixth Fleet left off.

Clearly new military policies were necessary under these changing strategic conditions. As America's principal regional surrogate power, Iran, fell at the end of the decade, and a direct Soviet threat to the Middle East suddenly reemerged a year later, an entirely new pattern of military involvement in the Middle East became necessary.

3. CENTCOM and the Emerging Pattern of US Military Interaction with the Middle East in the 1980s

The Evolution of the RDF Concept

The recognition by American planners that the United States required a special force for the new range of security threats in the Middle East in the late 1970s came in several stages during the Carter administration. First, in mid-1977 President Carter and his assistant for national security affairs, Zbigniew Brzezinski, ordered the National Security Council to conduct a review of overall US national security policy in light of changes that were appearing in Soviet strategy in an era of nuclear parity. In his memoirs, Brzezinski explains the motivation for his concern:

> I was convinced that our old doctrine was politically and psychologically credible only as long as America was in fact superior, and that it might not deter an opponent capable of conducting both a major or a more limited nuclear conflict and a significant conventional conflict or some combination thereof. Defense planning, I felt strongly, had to accommodate itself to this new reality and our defense doctrine and programs should be adjusted accordingly.[1]

The growth of Soviet strategic nuclear power, the enhancement of Soviet conventional capability, and improvements in Soviet strategic mobility, in Brzezinski's view, posed new challenges for the US military posture. Similar concerns were voiced in a study by the Office of the Secretary of Defense known as PRM-10 (Presidential Review Memorandum #10)[2]. A series of National Security Council decisions resulted from those initiatives that reformed US policies under conditions of what Brzezinski called "strategic equivalence;" one such result was PD-59 (Presidential Decision #59) that introduced major changes in US nuclear targeting. Regarding the Middle East, strategic equivalence had clearly created a situation where past policies of relying on the implied threat of escalating to general war for deterring direct Soviet attacks beyond the NATO area had become outdated. As a result, in August 1977 the NSC issued PD-18, which recommended a strategy of employing US general purpose forces in non-NATO situations, especially in the Middle East, Persian Gulf and Korea. PD-18 furthermore stipulated that these forces were to have the capability of operating independently of friendly basing and logistical support.[3]

The RDF thus owed its origins in part to the new perception in Washington of the shifting global balance of power. It also derived from a revision of US regional security policy as previously conceived by the Nixon Doctrine and the Twin Pillar Policy. Increased direct Soviet military involvement in Third World conflicts, as well as the utilization by the Soviets of Cuban proxy forces during the 1970s, created a new pattern of conflict that could not be left to regional powers alone. This perception was clearly reflected in the nervous reactions of the Saudi "pillar" — first, to the conflict in the Horn of Africa and then, in early 1979, to the attack of the Soviet-supported People's Democratic Republic of Yemen on its northern neighbor, the Yemen Arab Republic. Saudi concerns led to the first dispatch of US forces to Saudi Arabia since 1963: in January, an unarmed squadron of F-15s was deployed; this was followed in March by two E-3A AWACS[4]. If the Saudi pillar was jittery, the Iranian pillar had completely collapsed with the Islamic Revolution in Iran and the subsequent departure of the Shah in January 1979. William Quandt, the principal NSC staffer with responsibility for the Middle East in 1977-79, described the impact of the Shah's fall as follows:

> one lesson of Iran is likely to be that the United States cannot depend on regional surrogates and will have to rely more heavily on *its own forces* [emphasis added], on its own diplomacy, and on its own economic relations to protect its vital interests.[5]

A third stage in the development of the RDF concept came with the increasing appreciation of the danger of direct Soviet intervention in Iran. Certainly the most dramatic source of concern over direct Soviet military threats to the Middle East came from the Soviet invasion of Afghanistan in December 1979, which brought Soviet forces significantly closer to the Persian Gulf as well as to Pakistan. However, even prior to that event, there were indications of this newly expressed concern. During November 1978, the White House noted warnings from the USSR against US interference in Iranian internal affairs. It was not surprising therefore to see that, for the first time in many years, in January 1979 the new DOD FY 1980 Annual Report made mention of a new Middle Eastern scenario that American planners now had to take into account:

> If Soviet forces were to intervene, however, either in support of attacks by others or under pretext of defending the USSR from threats based in Iran, they could certainly overwhelm Iran's capability for defense...their intervention could well require a US response.[6]

The FY 1980 DOD Report at the same time attempted to play down this scenario in order not to be too alarmist. However, not long after the Soviet invasion of Afghanistan alarms did go off in Washington over the threat to Iran. In early 1980 the Soviets conducted a large-scale exercise testing their capabilities to invade Iran. Initially, American intelligence agencies monitoring Soviet communications were not sure whether they were witnessing an exercise or an actual invasion.[7] The cumulative impact of these events was to force American planners, for the first time since the early 1950s, to consider how to provide a localized defense of the Middle East from direct Soviet attacks.

A final stage in the development of the RDF concept was the emergence of a new geo-strategic definition for the Middle East-Persian Gulf area. The geographic span of the crises which alarmed the Carter administration in 1977-80 began with the Horn of Africa and stretched through the Yemens across the Arabian Peninsula to Iran, Afghanistan and Pakistan. Brzezinski called this area the "arc of crisis" and suggested that a new "security framework" be created throughout the area in which the US would reassert its power and influence. As the Middle East in the past had usually been thought of as ending in the east with Iran, a new term came into use after 1980: Southwest Asia encompassed the Horn of Africa, the Middle East-Persian Gulf, and parts of what had been known as South Asia. Beginning with the FY 1982 DOD Annual Report, the last such yearly report of the Carter administration, Southwest Asia became consistently referred to as the geographic focus of the Rapid Deployment Force. The actual boundaries of this enormous region would change in coming years and eventually become the area of responsibility of CENTCOM.

Several different force options came under consideration during 1979 for increasing the US military presence in the Southwest Asia region. From the beginning of the Iranian revolution through the Yemen border conflict, on repeated occasions the United States sought to increase its naval presence in the Arabian Sea through the movement of a carrier task force led by the USS Constellation.

Some of the difficulties encountered in diverting these forces from the Seventh Fleet in the Western Pacific suggested that a more permanent rather than ad hoc naval presence for the Indian Ocean was necessary. One option raised for this purpose was the establishment of a new US Fifth Fleet, as well as the dispatch, at regular intervals, of land-based combat aircraft to the Gulf states.[8] Another option raised by General Bernard Rogers, as he completed his task as Army chief of staff, was the creation of an Army-dominated "unilateral corps" for assignments in "the Persian Gulf, Middle East, Northeast Asia or anywhere outside the NATO-area."[9]

The ultimate form US force planning took in Southwest Asia certainly was a function of the interservice rivalries that raged in 1979 over the control of the rapid deployment mission. Strategic factors as well pointed to the need for a multiservice force to handle the range of threats — especially the growing Soviet threat to the Gulf. Secretary of Defense Harold Brown wrote in retrospect that at least three strategies were available for defending the oil-producing areas of the Gulf in the worst-case scenario of a direct Soviet overland attack.[10]

    a. Zagros Mountain Strategy — utilizing the hard terrain of Iran, this would involve holding a line along the Zagros mountains in southwestern Iran;

    b. Enclave Strategy — a less ambitious approach aspiring to hold only an enclave around the Iranian oil fields;

    c. Naval Strategy — aimed at defending the Iranian oil fields from the sea, it relied chiefly on US seapower, aircraft carriers and surface ships armed with cruise missiles and large naval guns.

Brown noted that a primarily naval strategy in Southwest Asia suffered from the constraints placed by geography on the deployment of carriers in the Gulf itself, especially in light of the threat they might face from hostile land-based aircraft. This analysis did not preclude an enhanced naval presence in the Indian Ocean, especially as a peacetime indicator of US strategic interests. Under wartime conditions, Brown preferred either the Enclave or Zagros Mountain strategies; he observed that both required land-based air forces as well as large ground forces. US rapid deployment capabilities for engaging the Soviets along the Zagros Mountain line, he wrote, would only be ready by the late 1980s.

The range of possible threats considered during 1979 that a new

US force would have to contend with — including direct Soviet overland attacks against Iran — meant that no single service or even a combination of two services could take sole responsibility for Southwest Asia. This was clearly evident when the Department of Defense finally created the Rapid Deployment Joint Task Force (RDJTF) in October 1979. The RDJTF, though only beginning as a planning and training organization within the US Readiness Command (REDCOM), included already existing units from all four services that were designated for the possible use of the RDJTF commander. These comprised at least three US Army divisions, three Marine amphibious brigades, up to three of the US Navy carrier task forces, and an undisclosed number of the US Air Force's tactical fighter wings. By virtue of its peacetime jurisdiction under REDCOM, the RDJTF came under the ultimate command of a US Army general. Once in the theater, the RDJTF's land-based operations in wartime could come under control of the Army-dominated European Command, while its sea-based operations could come under the Navy-dominated Pacific Command.[11]

In late November 1979, however, command of the RDJTF itself was given to Lt. General P.X. Kelley of the US Marine Corps. By March 1980, the headquarters of the RDJTF at MacDill Air Force Base in Florida were operational. Initially the RDJTF, in the spirit of PD-18, was intended for worldwide contingencies outside of the NATO area. However by July 1980 it focused its planning efforts on Southwest Asia only.[12] With this variety of forces, RDJTF Commander Kelley explained, US rapid deployment forces could be used flexibly in a range of scenarios on the spectrum of conflict from small force packages of a few light units to the entire force as a whole.[13]

Two other initiatives came to be associated with the establishment of the RDJTF. The first was the search for regional facilities. Even the very limited goal of increasing the US Navy's peacetime presence through extended deployment in the Indian Ocean required a more expanded use of airfields and ports along the rim of the Indian Ocean, especially since the nearest US supply bases were either in the Philippines or the Mediterranean. In addition, as the RDJTF planned for contending in wartime with the direct Soviet overland threat, special access arrangements had to be considered with the local states for supplying support facilities and staging areas for the substantial ground and air forces that the United States intended to deploy in the area. Agreements were secured in June 1980 with Kenya for the expanded use of the port of Mombasa by the US Navy as well as for access to lesser air and sea facilities. The same month a similar arrangement was made with Oman, after a delay caused by the unauthorized use of an Omani airfield during the April 24 hostage rescue attempt.[14] Under the agreement the United States set out to improve airfields on the island of Masira, in the remote Dhufar region at Thumarait, and at Khasab on the Musandam Peninsula adjacent to the Straits of Hormuz.[15] A third agreement was reached with Somalia in August 1980 for the increased use of its naval ports and airfields at Berbera and Mogadishu.[16]

These "facilities access agreements," as they came to be called, were clearly not base agreements. Each facility remained under the sovereign control of the host country. The United States took upon itself to expand and improve these facilities. The number of American personnel stationed as caretakers at each facility was intentionally held to between 15 and 100.[17] Activation of the facility for any contingency required the political approval of the host country.

The United States attempted to reach a similar understanding with Egypt for facilities access — but without a formal agreement. The US Air Force increased its use of Qena and Cairo West air bases. But plans to spend up to $400 million on upgrading the remote Egyptian Red Sea air base and port of Ras Banas into a major divisional rear staging area ran afoul when the US Congress refused to authorize funding in the absence of an explicit facilities access agreement.[18] The United States also attempted unsuccessfully to acquire facilities in Saudi Arabia. Nonetheless, a significant American military presence in Saudi Arabia was established in connection with the loan of AWACS aircraft and their support teams — during the Yemen crisis of March 1979 and again in September 1980 with the outbreak of the Iraq-Iran War — as well as in connection with the modernization of Saudi air facilities. The Saudi airbase modernization programs, though dating back to the early 1970s — before the conception of the RDJTF — nonetheless were planned on a scale that took into account possible access by friendly air forces.[19] Since these facilities improvements were financed by the Saudis themselves, tacit understandings could suffice regarding their use, and no written understandings became necessary to satisfy the US Congress. But whether Saudi-funded oversized facilities and compatible ammunition, fuel stocks, or spare parts would actually be made available to RDJTF in an emergency ultimately would be a function of a future Saudi political decision. In the absence of a written understanding, Saudi options appeared to be more open than those of Oman, Somalia and Kenya, although those states as well could conceivably restrict US use of their American-funded military infrastructures.

Other than the search for facilities, the RDJTF came to be associated with another initiative: the improvement of US strategic mobility. At sea, this entailed the initiation of three separate sealift programs:[20]

1. Near Term Prepositioning Ships (NTPS). Seven ships were immediately chartered to carry supplies, heavy equipment, fuel, and water for supporting one 16,500 man Marine amphibious brigade for 15 days of combat. With the Marines airlifted to the theater of operations where they would join up with their equipment, the brigade was expected to complete its deployment in six days. The NTPS Force eventually came to comprise some 17 ships: five for Marine ground and air units and 12 carrying ammunition, water, fuel and lubricants for the Army, Air Force and Navy.

2. Sea-Land Container Ships (SL-7). Six SL-7 high speed container ships were purchased in 1981 and modified with an improved roll-on/roll-off loading system. The SL-7 program taken together with airlift assets was expected to reduce deployment time of one mechanized infantry division from 30-35 days to 14. The ships were expected to be operational in the mid-1980s.

3. Maritime Prepositioning Ships (MPS). Fourteen new MPS ships were budgeted by the Department of Defense in 1979. The MPS Fleet was intended like the NTPs to marry up with airlifted Marines. MPS was conceived to carry the equipment for three Marine brigades. Eventually 13 MPS ships were acquired and deployed worldwide in three squadrons. When MPS-2 squadron came on station at Diego Carcia in December 1985, it replaced the Marine component of the NTPS Force. Most of the remaining 12 NTPS ships remained in Diego Garcia to serve the Air Force, Army, and Navy.

In the area of improved airlift less was accomplished initially in the Carter years than in the case of sealift. This was largely due to the protracted debate over whether the next generation military lift aircraft (the C-X, later C-17) was to have an inter-theater or intra-theater mission. Controversy over whether existing lines of production of transport aircraft could simply be extended for the needs of the RDJTF further dragged on the debate.

How the RDF concept evolved in the course of the 1980s, and the extent to which it represented a changed pattern of US military interaction with the Middle East, are considered systematically below.

From RDF to CENTCOM

By virtue of the limitations on US strategic mobility, the RDJTF upon its establishment was expected to be capable only of fielding a token force in Iran against an invading Soviet army; according to General Volney Warner, commander-in-chief of the US Readiness Command in 1980, the full strength of the RDJTF was expected to be realized only by 1985.[21] Between initial conception of the RDF and attainment of its anticipated deployable strength, several changes were brought in by the Reagan administration. Organizationally, on October 1, 1981 the RDJTF was transformed into a separate joint task force that reported to the National Command Authority (the president and the secretary of defense) through the JCS and not through the commander-in-chief of REDCOM. The RDJTF commander was given a clearly defined area of concern for planning purposes in Southwest Asia; the Army and Air Force units over which he would be given operational control were designated. These changes anticipated conversion of the RDJTF to a fully unified command that would draw together varied American defense efforts regarding Southwest Asia that had been divided among different unified commands, as indicated in Table 2.

In January 1983 this process culminated in the conversion of the RDJTF to the US Central Command and the RDJTF commander at Macdill Air Force Base in Florida to the Commander-in-Chief US Central Command (CINCCENT). Under CINCCENT were four component service commands as in other unified commands — as well as a unique multiservice special operations command (SOCENT). US Army forces CENTCOM (USARCENT) consisted of the Third US

Army at Ft. McPherson, Georgia; US CENTCOM Air Forces (USCENTAF) was commanded by the Ninth Air Force Commander at Shaw Air Force Base in South Carolina. CENTCOM naval assets came under USNAVCENT based in Pearl Harbor, Hawaii. The First Marine Amphibious Force as well as the highly mobile Seventh Marine Amphibious Brigade were designated as the CENTCOM Marine component.[22]

Table 2

Country-Wide Distribution of US Security Functions in Southwest Asia Before and After the Establishment of CENTCOM

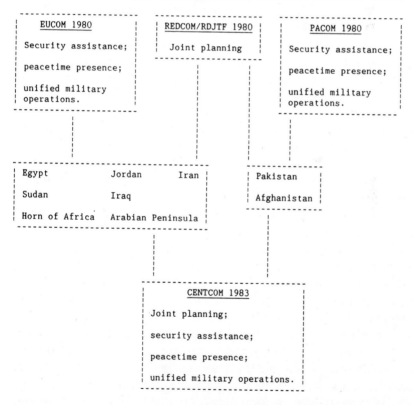

These organizational developments indicated that the Reagan administration not only accepted the RDF concept that was conceived by its predecessor but also sought to upgrade it. In the course of the 1980s several other modifications in the original RDF concept, that evolved as a result of changes in strategy or due to new regional conditions, became apparent in CENTCOM.

Subregional Focus: The CENTCOM Area of Responsibility (AOR)

With the advent of CENTCOM some subtle changes could be observed in the subregional focus of US defense efforts in the Middle East. The geographic buzzword for American strategic planning continued to be "Southwest Asia." When Southwest Asia was first referred to in the DOD FY 1982 report as the focus of RDJTF planning, like Brzezinski's "arc of crisis" it was depicted by the Defense Department as consisting of the countries of the Horn of Africa (Ethiopia, Somalia, Djibouti), Kenya in East Africa, the countries of the Arabian Peninsula, as well as Iraq, Iran, Afghanistan and Pakistan. Significantly, by the time CENTCOM was created in 1983 and its area of responsibility fixed, an expanded version of Southwest Asia had emerged that came to include Egypt, Sudan and Jordan. In all probability the former two were already added to the Southwest Asia concept under the RDJTF. Syria, Lebanon, and Israel remained in the area of responsibility of EUCOM. At sea the new CENTCOM borders placed only the Red Sea and the Persian Gulf within its AOR; beyond Bab al-Mandeb and the Straits of Hormuz the blue waters of the Arabian Sea and the western Indian Ocean were assigned to the US Pacific Command (PACOM) (see maps #2 and #3).

The reasons for the inclusion of Egypt in the CENTCOM AOR had already become apparent under the RDJTF. Despite the problems that were to develop over Ras Banas, Egypt became an important asset for RDJTF units during their Bright Star exercises in the Middle East. The first RDJTF regional exercise, *Bright Star 81*, was held near Cairo by a US air assault battalion in November 1980 in response to an invitation by President Anwar Sadat. While the far larger *Bright Star 82* regional exercise, held in late 1981, included Sudan, Somalia, and Oman as well, the largest US contingent (approximately 4,000 soldiers) was deployed to Egypt. Unexpected restrictions placed on the Marine amphibious maneuvers on the coast of Oman during *Bright Star 82* showed that Oman could not be completely depended on as a regional training ground in the future. By the time *Bright Star 83* was held in August-September 1983, Oman was omitted in favor of Egypt — which again hosted

Map 2. SOUTHWEST ASIA: RDJTF AREA OF CONCERN — 1980

SOURCE: DOD Annual Report FY 82

Map 3. SOUTHWEST ASIA: THE CENTCOM AREA OF RESPONSIBILITY — 1986

SOURCE: Adapted from Congressional Budget Office Report "Rapid Deployment Forces: Policy and Budgetory Implications" February 1983, DOD Annual Report FY 82, and Statement of General George Crist, CINCCENT, before the Senate Armed Services Committee March 11, 1986.

the largest contingent (5,500) — Somalia, and Sudan. With *Bright Star 85*, held in August 1985, Sudanese participation was precluded as a consequence of the April 6 coup against the pro-American Sudanese president, Ja'far al-Numayri. Egypt again was the location of the largest American contingent (9-10,000) during the exercise. Besides Somalia — and possibly Oman, whose participation was this time kept at an extremely low profile — a new state was added to Bright Star: Jordan.

In sum, beginning originally with the initiative of its president, Egypt's role in American preparations for the defense of Southwest Asia soon became a key component. By August 1987, Egypt alone was participating in *Bright Star 87*. In light of difficulties experienced elsewhere during CENTCOM exercises in the region, it is no wonder that Egypt was incorporated into Southwest Asia and into CENTCOM's AOR. Moreover, Egyptian use of Soviet weaponry and doctrine made the Egyptian Army an ideal training partner for US forces.

At the start of the US reflagging and convoy operations in mid-1987, a temporary modification was effectively made in CENTCOM's AOR. With the buildup of the US naval presence in the Gulf region divided between MIDEASTFOR — within the Straits of Hormuz and under the command of CENTCOM — and the US carrier and battleship battle groups in the Gulf of Oman and the Arabian Sea, that belonged to PACOM, command arrangements became excessively cumbersome. To unify the two forces, the JCS established a new "US Joint Task Force Middle East" (JTFME) commanded by a two-star Navy rear admiral, who reported directly to the commander-in-chief of CENTCOM. With PACOM's carrier force "chopped" to CENTCOM, the latter had effectively extended its maritime boundary beyond the Straits of Hormuz.

CENTCOM's Conception of the Threat to Southwest Asia

Six years after the Soviet invasion of Afghanistan, CENTCOM continued to prepare for the worst-case scenario of renewed Soviet expansionism within its area of responsibility. In a statement before the Senate Armed Services Committee in March 1986, General George Crist, Commander-in-Chief of CENTCOM, defined its objectives in a way that clearly placed its anti-Soviet mission at the top of the list of its concerns:[23]

- maintain an increased US military presence to deter Soviet aggression and counter Soviet efforts to gain power and hegemony in the region;
- strive to reduce the potential for regional conflict, enhance regional stability, and promote a framework for regional defense cooperation;
- maintain access to and unhindered use of Persian Gulf oil resources.

According to Crist, the CENTCOM AOR was for Soviet strategic interests no less than "the highest priority target for the expansion of Soviet influence in the Third World." As will be shown when its force structure is analyzed below, the planned increase in Army ground forces under CENTCOM, in comparison with the RDJTF, indicated that it still took its anti-Soviet mission seriously. Moreover, in addition to the Soviet threat to Iran, CENTCOM was also concerned with a spillover of the war in Afghanistan into Pakistan.

Other recent US assessments of the direct Soviet threat in this region have been far less urgent than those of CENTCOM. Leading figures in the Reagan administration, including the late CIA director, William Casey, played down the prospects of any direct Soviet challenge to Iran.[24] Even the Department of Defense's own *Soviet Military Power* stated in its 1987 edition that the Soviet Southern Strategic Theatre (TVD) — that commands forces facing eastern Turkey, Iran, Afghanistan and Pakistan — "currently has low priority for Soviet planners."[25] These more relaxed views of the Soviet threat could be supported by an analysis of the relatively slower quantitative and qualitative growth of Soviet forces in the Southern USSR in comparison with Soviet forces deployed against NATO and the PRC (Table 3).

Moreover, whereas most of the Soviet ground forces facing NATO and the PRC are known to be in a relatively high state of readiness, the IISS has reported over the last 15 years that most of the divisions in the military districts that today constitute the Southern TVD are category three divisions: they are at about one-quarter strength and contain obsolete equipment.

Yet a static view of the Soviet force structure in the Southern TVD does not take into account Soviet capabilities to reinforce or rotate these lower-grade divisions by using the Soviet rail system and other means of internal communication.[26] Moreover, looking to the future, the Soviet force posture in the Southern TVD could well be improved as an unintended consequence of arms control agreements in Europe. President Reagan's Commission on an integrated long-term US strategy has warned that a NATO-Warsaw Pact conventional arms control agreement that shifts Soviet forces from Europe to east of the Urals would leave them 830 nautical miles from southwestern Iran (in comparison, US forces relocated from Western Europe to North America would be 6,400 nautical miles away). Under such conditions, the Soviets could best assert their comparative advantage in geography against the Middle East. The commission not surprisingly does not dismiss the future threat of the Soviet Union to the Gulf region:

> The turbulence of the region, the importance of its oil to Western countries for the foreseeable future, the severe limitations of countervailing forces in the region — all these factors combine to make it plausible that Soviet leaders might seize an opportunity to intervene — for example, by taking advantage of an "invitation" to support a new revolutionary regime.[27]

As the future of Sino-Soviet ties is not only dependent on the problem of Kampuchea or the Soviet occupation of Afghanistan, but most importantly on the reduction of Soviet force levels on the Chinese border, future Sino-Soviet understandings could also lead to a Soviet buildup in the Southern TVD in a fashion similar to the NATO-Warsaw Pact agreement described above.

Table 3

Soviet Divisional Ground Strength in Different Theaters*

	1971/72	1975/76	1980/81	1986/87*	% Change
Southern USSR	28	23	24	30	+ 6%
European USSR & Eastern Europe	91	94	97	100	+ 9%
Sino-Soviet border	33	43	46	53	+38%

* includes four divisions in Afghanistan

Source: IISS

As is evident in the second of its objectives listed above, CENTCOM has by no means been oblivious to the problem of regional conflicts. Since its inception, CENTCOM closely followed developments in the Iran-Iraq War; it assumed control of the USAF AWACS monitoring Saudi Arabia's Eastern Defense Sector since October 1980. CENTCOM's operational command as well as the US contingent in the Multinational Force and Observers (MFO) over-saw the Egypt-Israel peace treaty from the Egyptian Sinai. One month after CENTCOM's establishment, one of its first missions was the dispatch of four AWACS to Egypt in order to monitor Libyan air movements for the Egyptian Air Force, after the US received warnings that Libya planned an air attack on Sudan that was to be followed by a coup attempt. USAF AWACS and support-ing aircraft under CENTCOM command returned to Egypt in March 1984 after a Libyan bomber attack on the Sudanese city of Omdurman. Four months later, when the US was called upon to assist both Egypt and Saudi Arabia in taking countermeasures against the mining of the Red Sea, CENTCOM became involved again. In 1986, as US merchant ships in the Persian Gulf faced stop and search operations by the Iranian Navy, MIDEASTFOR under CENTCOM's naval command took measures to discourage the Iranians.[28] Thus while CENTCOM continued to plan for the worst-case scenario of a massive Soviet overland attack, the AWACS, the MFO and the small naval contingents that made up CENTCOM's modest peacetime regional presence took an active role in regional security affairs.

Moreover, the US reflagging and convoy operations of mid-1987 illustrate that a certain degree of interplay exists between the Soviet and regional threats that CENTCOM was designed to meet. Early critics of the reflagging scheme argued that while the administration claimed it was acting to block the spread of Soviet influence, US forces in the Gulf were in fact directed against Iran; some observers even saw mutual US-Soviet interests in supporting Iraq and preventing an Iranian victory in the war. What had in fact occurred in the course of 1986 leading up to the Kuwaiti request for US and Soviet tanker protection, was that a regional conflict — the Iran-Iraq War — intensified past the point where a local state could guarantee its security alone or by alignment with a regional grouping. This raised the issue of who would become the state's external protector. Once the Soviet Union became a candidate for that role, the United States was compelled to preempt and assume the role itself. In short, a regional conflict had opened the door for superpower rivalry. The US found itself drawn into containing a regional conflict before it provided new opportunities for a significantly expanded Soviet position in the Gulf. CENTCOM's essentially anti-Soviet purpose had thus not changed, although rather than stopping the Soviets physically its forces were now being used to block them politically.

CENTCOM's Force Structure

Under the Reagan administration, the overall size of the force dedicated to the rapid deployment mission grew considerably — especially its Army component. The changing force structures of the RDJTF and CENTCOM along the course of the 1980s are shown in Table 4.[29]

The total number of personnel that could be designated for the RDJTF in 1981 and CENTCOM in 1983 was around 220,000. In addition to the forces added by 1986, the Reagan administration planned on reaching a two-divisional strength Marine Force as well as a total of ten tactical fighter wings by 1989, thus bringing the total number of personnel associated with CENTCOM to 440,000.[30] In all likelihood, cutbacks in US defense spending in 1987 would complicate the achievement of these originally antici-pated force levels.

In peacetime, CENTCOM has no control over this enormous force list. When the Army and Air Force components of these forces are in the continental US (CONUS), they fell under REDCOM's jurisdiction until 1987, and its successor command thereafter. Navy and Marine units are connected to LANTCOM or PACOM depending on their location. Besides controlling its headquarters at Macdill Air Force base in Florida, CENTCOM has command over those minimal US forces stationed in its AOR: the five ships of MIDEASTFOR, the MFO, and the Saudi Arabian-based US AWACS. Moreover, CENTCOM's complete force list was not designed for lesser contingencies, such as internal subversion or intraregional inter-state wars, in Southwest Asia. CENTCOM was not conceived to replace the Shah of Iran as gendarme of the Gulf; US national security policy in 1987 remained cautious about the use of American forces in lesser contingencies:[31]

> ....For military contingencies not involving the Soviet Union, however, the United States looks primarily to the nations

Table 4

The Growth of the Rapid Deployment Force Structure Over the 1980s

	RDJTF 1981		CENTCOM 1983		CENTCOM 1986
1	Airborne Division	1	Airborne Division	1	Airborne Division
1	Air Assault Division	1	Air Assault Division	1	Air Assault Division
1	Mechanized Infantry Division	1	Mechanized Infantry Division	1	Mechanized Infantry Division
1	Air Cavalry Brigade	1	Air Cavalry Brigade	2	Infantry Divisions
3 1/3	Total Army Divisions	3 1/3	Total Army Divisions	5	Total Army Divisions
1	Marine Amphibious Force	1	Marine Amphibious Force	1	Marine Amphibious Force
1	Marine Amphibious Brigade	1	Marine Amphibious Brigade	1	Marine Amphibious Brigade
1 1/3	Total Marine Divisions	1 1/3	Total Marine Divisions	1 1/3	Total Marine Divisions
4 2/3	Total Ground Force Divisions	4 2/3	Total Ground Force Divisions	6 1/3	Total Ground Force Divisions
5	Tactical Fighter Wings	7	Tactical Fighter Wings	7	Tactical Fighter Wings
2	Strategic Bomber Squadrons	2	Strategic Bomber Squadrons	2	Strategic Bomber Squadrons
3	carrier battle groups	3	carrier battle groups	3	carrier battle groups
1	surface action group	1	surface action group	1	surface action group
5	maritime patrol squadrons	5	maritime patrol squadrons	5	maritime patrol squadrons

involved to provide for their own defense.

Direct involvement of US military forces is a *last resort* [emphasis added] to be undertaken only when clear political objectives have been established, our political will is clear, and appropriate military capabilities are available.

Nevertheless, CENTCOM forces still have a greater role to play in regional security than US forces did under the Nixon Doctrine. First, even CENTCOM's small peacetime presence, when taken together with PACOM's forward deployed carriers in the Indian Ocean, serve to deter certain local conflicts. While not influencing the outcome of the Iran-Iraq War, these forces have been used to deter Iran from considering the spread of the war to the Gulf states. Secondly, in regional conflicts CENTCOM can fill gaps in the military capabilities of states friendly to the US. The assistance provided by US-controlled AWACS to the Egyptian and Saudi air forces best illustrates this function. Finally CENTCOM, by seeking to promote regional defense cooperation, can actively assist local allies like the Jordanian RDF that may intervene in regional crises.

Even in an anti-Soviet contingency, it must be stated that however the force structures of the RDJTF or CENTCOM appear in the various DOD annual reports, these troop lists are by no means certain. Secretary Weinberger has admitted that many of CENT-COM's designated forces are "dual or even triple-hatted" — that is, they have also been designated for missions in other theaters.[32] RDF critic Jeffrey Record noted in 1984 that for the Reagan administration to fulfill its declared responsibilities in Southwest Asia without jeopardizing its ability to reinforce NATO-Europe, the US would have had to increase its 1983-Army active division strength from 16 to at least 20.[33] Col. John M. Collins (ret.), senior defense analyst for the Congressional Research Service at the Library of Congress, looking at the Army's 16-active division force in 1980, noted that five divisions were already assigned to EUCOM and two divisions to PACOM (one of which was held in theater reserve in Hawaii).[34] Of the nine remaining divisions in the continental United States (CONUS), two had "strings attached" to EUCOM for NATO reinforcement, while another six were necessary to hold in reserve for specialized training and overseas rotation. Under "worst case" conditions, according to which international conditions allow no tampering with EUCOM and PACOM reinforcements, only one US Army active division was calculated available for a RDJTF/CENTCOM contingency. Under "best case" conditions, PACOM'S theater reserves in Hawaii as well as EUCOM's CONUS forces could be used for rotation and training, freeing up to four Army divisions for use in Southwest Asia.

Similar calculations were made for the Air Force, Marines, and Navy as well. Even in 1980 under worst case conditions the Air Force had 26 squadrons of attack fighters available for a non-EUCOM/PACOM contingency. These could adequately cover CENTCOM's end of decade force list of seven wings (21 squadrons). The situation with the Marines and Navy was more problematic. Under worst-case conditions in 1979-80 none of the Marines' three divisions or the Navy's carrier task forces could be made available. Even in 1986 it was becoming difficult for the US to maintain simultaneously a peacetime carrier presence in both the Mediterranean and the Arabian Sea; in January the shift of the USS Saratoga from waters near Iran to Libya left the Gulf region without carrier coverage.[35] The expected growth of the Navy's active carrier force from 13 for most of the 1980s to 15 by 1989-90, should help relieve this problem. The Marine Corps is not expected to undergo significant growth, so that limitations on its use could be expected to be felt in worst case multi-theater crises scenarios in the future as well.

Figures on the US Army's limited ability to cover simultaneous crises are probably the most significant ones to look at for determining whether the US Military Establishment could safely afford to activate RDJTF/ CENTCOM in any given period. The US Army's ground forces are the least mobile military component among the US armed services; they cannot easily be shifted to another theater should a suddenly more urgent crisis elsewhere demand a redeployment of US forces. In other words, the Army's ground forces are the most difficult element in CENTCOM's combat force structure to assign to Southwest Asia without injuring other commitments. Hence, only if sufficient ground divisions can be safely assigned to CENTCOM will that force's principal operational limiting factor be removed.

The Department of Defense has attempted to tackle the problem of the US Army's limited active divisional strength in recent years without increasing the Army's overall number of personnel, in part by improving the Army's mobility though the creation of Army light divisions. Unlike the standard American mechanized infantry division that consists of approximately 16,000 soldiers, the new light division is made up of only about 10,000 soldiers with no supporting tank units or large calibre (203mm and 155mm) artillery. In 1986 the United States was in the process of activating or converting five divisions in the "light" configuration: the 7th Infantry Division at Fort Ord, California; the 25th Infantry Division in Hawaii; the 6th Infantry Division based in Alaska, the 10th Mountain Division at Fort Drum, New York; and the 29th Infantry Division at Fort Belvoir, Virginia.[36]

The light division has helped the US Army increase its active divisional strength. In 1968, at the height of the Vietnam buildup, the US Army reached an active divisional strength of 19 1/3 divisions. This number plummeted to 12 2/3 divisions in 1972 and rose to 16 divisions by 1976; the Army's active divisional strength then remained constant through 1984.[37] By 1987, the US Army was able to build up to a strength of 18 active divisions; its former reserve strength of eight divisions was also increased to 10 divisions.[38]

Certain weaknesses existed behind the increased numbers. First, as of 1984, US strategy had more ambitious plans for the ground defense of NATO-Europe: DOD set as its goal to increase US forces in Europe to 10 Army divisions within 10 days of a decision to reinforce. Thus instead of having seven divisions tied to Europe as calculated by Collins in 1980, the United States now had three more.

A second weakness evident in both the 6th Light Infantry Division and the 10th Mountain Division was that only five of the nine infantry battalions in each came from the active forces; both divisions were assigned reserve "roundout" brigades.[39] The tactical support structure of some of the Army's active divisions also relies increasingly on reserve components so as "to increase the Army's ability to support the United States Central Command (USCENTCOM) without drawing down on forces needed for Europe," according to the DOD's FY '87 Annual Report.[40]

The light division was especially conceived, however, for improving the Army's high speed air-deployable mobility. Taking the payload of the USAF's C-141A as a measure (75,400 lbs.), a regular Army mechanized infantry division has been calculated to require some 3000 sorties. Even the lighter 101st Air Assault Division would need over a thousand sorties to deploy; the 82nd Airborne Division would need only 750 sorties. The light division was planned to be deployable in only 500 such sorties.[41] Because of its reduced firepower and land mobility, it has been argued that the Army's light infantry would be of little use in the European theater against Soviet mechanized divisions. It might equally be argued that the light division would not even be appropriate in Southwest Asia in an anti-Soviet scenario; the light division would seem most appropriate in low or middle intensity conflicts against Soviet client states. However, if the United States chooses to delay a Soviet advance in the Zagros Mountains, light divisions utilizing Iran's harsh geography of narrow mountain passes could seriously impede invading Soviet forces suffering from severe maneuverability constraints. In short, light divisions might be especially useful in Southwest Asia; that they might be less useful in Europe only increases the likelihood of their being available to CENTCOM rather than EUCOM in an emergency.

The growth of the army component of CENTCOM's combat force structure in comparison to what was originally associated with RDJTF implies a possible shift in US strategy in Southwest Asia: from deterrence to defense. When the original smaller RDJTF was put together, the US admittedly had no chance of defending even an enclave around the oil-producing south of Iran from a Soviet ground attack. A Defense Department study prepared in 1979 determined that within a 30-day period, the US could field a force of 20,000 troops in Iran, while the Soviets could field 100,000 or more.[42] The original RDF was more of a "tripwire" force. But unlike the American "tripwire" in West Berlin it was not prepositioned in place; instead, it had to be rapidly introduced to Iran before the Soviets seized positions of vital importance to the West. Brzezinski gives some credence to this view of the early RDF:

> It is true that when the commitment to the security of the Persian Gulf was made the United States was not in a position to meet the Soviet Union on the ground, so to speak, matching man for man or tank for tank. Geography and logistical complexities made that impossible....The point of both the Truman Doctrine and what later came to be called the Carter Doctrine was to make the Soviet Union aware of the fact that the intrusion of Soviet armed forces into an area of vital importance to the United States would precipitate an engagement *with* the United States and that the United States would then be free to choose the manner in which it would respond. In fact in our private contingency preparations, I

made the point of instructing the Defense Department to develop options involving both 'horizontal and vertical escalation' in the event of a Soviet military move toward the Persian Gulf.[43]

In Brzezinski's formulation, the RDJTF was to be put in place so as to signal the USSR that the Gulf region was of vital importance to the US. With even a small tripwire force, the US could add credibility to its application of extended deterrence to Southwest Asia.[44]

In all probability this early RDJTF strategy was more of a product of necessity than design; with limited mobility assets and an undeveloped regional logistic structure there was little more the US could do in 1980. Moreover, Brzezinski had already recognized in 1977 that under conditions of nuclear parity new conventional means were necessary for deterring the USSR in non-NATO regions. Vertical escalation in the Gulf region may have been an option for the 1950s; it was unrealistic for the 1980s. Horizontal escalation strategies were considered in the early years of the Reagan administration, but then declined in popularity in the American defense community except in the US Navy. Critics accurately pointed out the problem of identifying equivalent Soviet assets abroad that the West could threaten: could the West's principal oil reserves be compared with Nicaragua, Cuba, or North Vietnam?[45] Furthermore, horizontal escalation strategies favored the USSR rather than the US, since the Soviets enjoyed conventional superiority and geographic proximity and could thus choose from a number of western assets along the Eurasian land mass without drawing down their forces for missions in higher priority theaters. In short, the enlargement of the RDF under CENTCOM for the purpose of having a real defense option in Southwest Asia appears consistent with the general strategic environment of the 1980s. Moreover, the expansion of CENTCOM's force structure raised the nuclear threshold in the Middle East, as it gave greater credibility to the chances for conventional defense.

A review of CENTCOM's force structure would be incomplete, especially for describing the transition from the RDJTF, without looking at developments in its strategic mobility assets. Strategic airlift remains a critical, though expensive, US force projection mission, especially if CENTCOM seeks to field a force in a given location in its AOR before the Soviets arrive and create a fait accompli. The Department of Defense established in 1981 in the

Congressionally-Mandated Mobility Study that the US set a goal of 66 million-ton-miles per day (MTM/D) of airlift capacity to meet its worldwide missions. This was based on an estimate that the US would need to deliver by air 8,000 tons of troops, equipment and supplies for each day of a Persian Gulf contingency and 19,000 tons per day for a conflict in NATO-Europe. In 1980, the US had less than 30 MTM/D. With the 1982 decision to add 50 C-5Bs to the fleet of 70 C-5As, add 44 KC-10 tanker/transport aircraft, and modify 19 747 aircraft associated with the Civilian Reserve Air Fleet (CRAF), the United States was able to increase its capacity to 46 MTM/D in 1986; this was expected to reach 48.5 MTM/D by mid-1988. The resulting airlift shortfall of 17.5 MTM/D is expected to be met by a fleet of 180 C-17 cargo aircraft that is planned to become fully operational by the end of the century.[46]

Sealift has been more of a success story than airlift. By mid-1988 the United States planned to have tripled its 1981 sealift capacity. The same 1981 Congressionally-Mandated Mobility Study quantified US sealift needs at 4.6 million deadweight tons of dry cargo. By 1987 America already had 4.2 million deadweight tons. This had been accomplished by completion of the SL-7 Fast Sealift Fleet program of eight ships in 1986, the phasing in of three Maritime Prepositioned Ships (MPS) squadrons (each carrying between one-quarter and one-fifth of the supplies needed for 30 days of combat by a 16,500-man Marine amphibious brigade), and the enlargement of the Ready Reserve Force's dry cargo merchant fleet from 20 vessels in 1980 to 93 vessels in 1987.[47] Both airlift and sealift programs have generally received DOD and congressional support — debates over the C-17 notwithstanding — because improved strategic mobility is essential for improving US ground force deployability in all theaters, not just in Southwest Asia. The rapid deployment mission to the Gulf thus sparked mobility programs that were badly needed for the reinforcement of NATO-Europe and Korea as well.

Taking the improvements in the size of CENTCOM's combat forces as well as the growth of US strategic mobility, how have US rapid deployment capabilities improved? Thomas L. McNaugher has calculated that in FY 1984, when CENTCOM had just inherited the forces of the RDJTF, the United States needed between six and seven weeks to deploy a force consisting of one Marine division and three Army divisions. Taking programed mobility assets, he estimated that by FY 1988, the US would need five weeks to get one

Marine division and four Army divisions to the Gulf area. Looking at the most mobile forces alone in these calculations, in FY 1984 it took four weeks to deploy a Marine division and the 82nd Airborne Division. By FY 1988 these two divisions could be in place in two weeks time. Deployment times could be improved with sufficient strategic warning. For example prepositioned ships, whether stationed in Diego Garcia or the United States, could head out even earlier for the Persian Gulf.[48]

Would these deployment schedules be sufficient for challenging the Soviet advance? As Joshua Epstein has pointed out, even granting the Soviet Army a fantastic rate of advance of 33 1/3 km/day, it would take the first heavily armed units of advancing Soviet columns 30 days to cover the 1000-kilometer distance from Soviet Azerbaijan through the Zagros Mountains to the head of the Gulf.[49] Should the US acquire the regional basing needed to conduct a successful early air interdiction campaign or deploy special operations forces in order to close off mountain passes and demolish bridges, it might have a month to prepare the defense of a line significantly north of the Gulf in mountainous Iranian Kurdistan. Of course, a Soviet move to the Gulf from Afghanistan would cut distances from 1000 to approximately 400 kilometers. For such an option to be workable, improved subjugation of the Afghan resistance would be a necessary prerequisite. In short, deployment times and distances permit consideration of an American defense of part of Iran from an assault in the north by the late 1980s. Whether local conditions in Iran or in neighboring states would permit such deployments, and how Soviet counter-strategies might affect their prosecution, are of course different matters entirely.

CENTCOM and the Relative Strategic Importance of the Middle East

The Carter Doctrine of January 1980 defined "any attempt to gain control of the Persian Gulf region" as "an assault on the *vital* interests of the United States of America" (emphasis added). Deterrence of any further Soviet moves in Southwest Asia required an unambiguous statement of the importance of the region to the US. By defining its interests in the Middle East as "vital," the US appeared to be putting the region on a par with Europe and the Far East. Brzezinski has acknowledged that this was the essential result of the new policy:

> The cumulative effect of the events and decisions of 1979-80
> was a strategic revolution in America's global position. Until
> the 1970s, U.S. foreign policy was anchored on the principle
> of interdependence with Western Europe, and then later with
> the Far East. The Middle East was viewed as a semi-neutral
> zone sealed off from Soviet power by a protective belt
> composed of Turkey, Iran, and Pakistan with a neutral
> Afghanistan providing a buffer....However, the collapse of
> Iran and the Soviet move into Afghanistan, preceded by the
> unimpeded Soviet military intrusion into Ethiopia and South
> Yemen, created an urgent security problem for the region as a
> whole prompted by 1980 formal US recognition of the
> security interdependence of three, instead of two, zones of
> central strategic importance to the United States: Western
> Europe, the Far East and the Middle East.[50]

Thus clearly, by declaration as well as by its military policies, the
Carter administration intended to revise traditional American
global strategic priorities. How the United States would cover this
added commitment without a substantial buildup of its conventional forces, Carter left to his successor to solve.

The Reagan administration in its first term accepted the new
obligations for Southwest Asia. Secretary of Defense Caspar
Weinberger in September 1981 not only justified the establishment
of the RDJTF and its mission, but called for its expansion. The
implications of this ambitious program for US capabilities to
reinforce NATO were not regarded as pressing since the threats
facing Europe and Northeast Asia were perceived to be less urgent
than those facing the Gulf region.[51] The Reagan administration
strove unsuccessfully to get its European allies to make up for the
forces it was planning to shift to the RDJTF. In 1982, as CENTCOM
critic Jeffrey Record has noted, Weinberger appeared to be putting
forward a planned global strategy that made no distinction among
American priorities:

> Our long-term goal is to be able to meet the demands of a
> worldwide war including concurrent reinforcement of
> Europe, deployment to Southwest Asia and the Pacific, and
> support for other areas...our long range goal is to be capable
> of defending all theatres simultaneously.[52]

The Department of Defense made no pretense about its capabilities in 1982 to execute what Record has accurately described as a 3

1/2 war strategy; these were long-term goals. Nonetheless, the strategy indicated that for planning purposes the US continued to accept what Brzezinski described as a "strategic revolution in America's global position" — the elevation of the Middle East to a level of importance comparable to Europe and the Pacific.

Developments in the second term of the Reagan administration indicate a more sober approach regarding American capabilities to cover three strategic theaters. This moderation of administration attitudes was not so much reflected in a changed assessment of US capabilities as in a debate over the necessary conditions that had to be met before taking any decision to employ American forces abroad. The strictest school of thought about the use of force was that of Secretary of Defense Caspar Weinberger. In an address to the National Press Club in late November 1984, Weinberger outlined his six criteria or tests to be applied when the use of American combat forces was under consideration: (a) the interest to be defended is deemed vital; (b) force must be applied with the intention of winning; (c) clearly defined political and military objections must be set forth; (d) forces deployed must be appropriate for US objectives in size, composition, and disposition; (e) reasonable assurance must exist that the mission will have the support of Congress and public opinion, and finally, (f) the commitment of US forces to combat should be a last resort.[53]

Weinberger's six tests were declared in the aftermath of the US presence in Lebanon and at the time of a deepening American involvement in Central America. They were not final presidential policy — something of a debate emerged at the time between the secretary of defense and Secretary of State George Shultz over the use of force in US counterterrorist strategy. Yet in light of Secretary Weinberger's strong support for the US reflagging and convoy mission in the Gulf in mid-1987, the six tests reveal a great deal about administration thinking regarding Southwest Asia as a zone of American strategic interest. There could have been good reasons for arguing a declining US interest in the Gulf region during Reagan's second term: the bogged-down Soviet occupation of Afghanistan did not appear any longer to be the first step in a Russian race to the Straits of Hormuz; increases of non-OPEC Western Hemisphere production of oil had greatly depreciated the relative importance of Persian Gulf oil to the US; and shifts in the American economy from heavy energy-intensive industry to lighter forms of manufacturing as well as improving gas economy performance in the American automobile industry had lowered anticipated future demand for imported oil. Most of all, as the Iran-Iraq War continued to rage — even spilling over into the Gulf itself — without affecting either the price or availability of oil, there appeared to be little reason to focus on the Gulf as a likely zone of American military intervention.

Despite these political-economic developments of recent years, even the cautious secretary of defense argued that in 1987 the Gulf region remained a region where *vital* national interests were at stake. Weinberger's reasoning was based on facts that were not subject to annual change, but had held true, he explained, for decades past. It was the objective of the US to "deny Soviet access/influence in a region which could threaten free world access to regional oil resources" as well as to assure the "stability and security of the Gulf states." Weinberger was not bothered by the relatively small role of Persian Gulf oil in US oil consumption; he noted that only six percent of US consumption in 1986 originated from the area. His assessment of the importance of the region — and hence the necessity to deploy US forces — was based not on oil production or consumption statistics, but rather "on the fact that seventy percent (70%) of the world's proven oil reserves are in the Gulf region."[54]

In short, while the US secretary of defense appeared to establish criteria for the use of force overseas that were so rigorous that any conflict short of a major world war might not merit American intervention, nevertheless Southwest Asia and the Persian Gulf in particular remained a vital American mission that received US military support when the "test" had to be made. While CENT-COM's critics might have had some basis for arguing that US interests in the Gulf were in decline, the American decision to protect reflagged Kuwaiti tankers reestablished the Gulf region as a vital American interest seven years after the Carter Doctrine. While CENTCOM's naval presence after mid-1987 was aimed against Iran and not the USSR, it was the specific threat of an expanded Soviet role in the Gulf that prompted the Reagan administration to undertake its commitments to Kuwait. Even if Moscow was having problems digesting Afghanistan, the US had been alerted again to Soviet interest in Southwest Asia.

4. Regional Responses to CENTCOM Strategies

While CENTCOM's AOR stretches from Kenya to Afghanistan, the territories most critical for the successful prosecution of the two principal rapid deployment missions — stopping the Soviets in Iran and keeping open the flow of oil — are located in the immediate proximity of the Persian Gulf itself. Most overt academic discussions of possible CENTCOM strategies focus on the critical initial role to be played by land-based airpower — within striking distance of northern Iran — in slowing down any Soviet advance in the natural bottlenecks formed by the Iranian mountain passes. Later, the deployment of US ground forces could be expected to require large nearby facilities for stationing the extensive support forces that would help sustain American combat troops. Should such a crisis arise, moreover, it is doubtful that CINCCENT would continue to command its forces from 8,000 miles away at Macdill Air Force Base in Florida or even from the small advanced headquarters set up on MIDEASTFOR's Flagship, the USS LaSalle. It would in all likelihood seek a regional command facility.

These basing considerations all relate to actual warfighting scenarios, but assured access to regional facilities might prove to be critical for pre-war deterrence, too. During the month-long Soviet mobilization time, *before the Soviet border is crossed*, US forces in place would serve best to dissuade any Soviet leadership that seemed to doubt American resolve in such an operationally difficult environment. Even in non-Soviet lesser scenarios — e.g., an Iranian ground threat to Kuwait — it has been generally acknowledged that the most persuasive US deterrent forces in pre-war or non-war deployments have been land-based aircraft and ground forces.[1]

For all of these reasons, the receptiveness of local states — particularly in the Persian Gulf — to CENTCOM's operational needs is practically a prerequisite for it to accomplish its original objective. The sixty-four thousand dollar question for CENTCOM is whether local states will grant it use of their facilities and under what circumstances.

CENTCOM openly acknowledges that this remains one of its problems:

We need access for exercises, for prepositioning and, in the worst case, for bases to support warfighting....However, the realities of the political situation make it difficult for the US to reach agreements to use and modernize air and sea facilities at many locations. Tensions between host nations; the Arab-Israel dispute; fear of ostracism; differing perceptions of the threat; and questions relating to upgrading costs, rental fees, and sharing of financial burdens all serve to complicate the access issue.[2]

CENTCOM has pursued several strategies to solve the access problem. First, it has attempted to reach understandings with a number of countries in order to ensure "that one country does not have veto power over US options...."[3] Secondly, CENTCOM has pursued an active political-military strategy with each state in its AOR that seeks to identify its military needs, to assess what security assistance might be necessary and to propose specific logistics programs, joint exercises, planning and finally "coalition activities with US military forces" that suit CENTCOM's strategic needs.[4] CENTCOM has received support from the Department of State — which has pursued a parallel initiative called a "Diplomatic Strategy to Achieve US National Security Objectives in SWA."[5] Third, as noted in the previous chapter, a principal US national security objective has been set as the promotion of a "framework for regional defense cooperation" in the CENTCOM AOR. Along with the enhanced capabilities of individual states, this is viewed by CINCCENT as a "significant force multiplier...should we be required to fight."[6]

In short, CENTCOM has sought to establish some kind of political-military consensus with the states in its AOR in order to assure its own military effectiveness. CENTCOM commanders often compare their situation to that of EUCOM in Western Europe, almost jealously pointing out the relative ease with which the US can carry out its NATO obligations within a prepositioned communications structure, and with a regional headquarters in the area of operations. EUCOM's task is made easier by the fact that a certain minimal coalition consensus preceded its military mission assignment. CENTCOM is seeking to create that coalition after being assigned its task. In the geostrategically critical Gulf area itself, this in effect has involved US relations with the only active regional defense organization in the entire CENTCOM AOR — the Gulf Cooperation Council (GCC). It has also involved bilateral ties with those regional states most critical to American strategy.

In the following pages, the receptiveness of this organization, as well as that of other states in Southwest Asia, to CENTCOM's various missions will be considered. The focus of the analysis will be on two issues: (a) regional attitudes toward the USSR and the Soviet threat, and (b) regional attitudes toward handling intraregional and internal threats. In both cases stress will be placed on regional attitudes toward cooperation with the US. This will entail not only consideration of public statements, but also the reaction of local states to actual crises, particularly the beginning of the Tanker War in 1984, within the larger framework of the Iran-Iraq War.

GCC Conceptions of Regional Security

When the GCC was officially established by the rulers of Saudi Arabia, Kuwait, Bahrain, Qatar, the UAE and Oman in May 1981, its member states were moved by very different concerns. Some even differed over the very purpose of the organization. As early as 1978, as a reaction to the brief formation of the Syrian-Iraqi axis after the Camp David accords, Kuwait had sought to promote closer cooperation among the Gulf states.[7] By 1981, with that axis broken and Iraq at war with Iran, Kuwait discounted the need to coordinate against external security threats and preferred to see the new organization move in the direction of economic and political cooperation. Oman, both politically and geographically at the "other end" of the GCC, sought to compensate for the withdrawal of the Iranian anti-insurgency forces that had operated from 1973 to 1979 against PDRY-supported guerrillas in the province of Dhufar.[8] Oman sought a means to counterbalance Soviet military and economic support for the regime in Aden. It proposed that the GCC members establish a joint naval force to protect the Gulf, unify their air defense systems, and hold joint military maneuvers.[9] Saudi Arabia, having undergone several major internal disturbances in 1979-80, proposed to increase cooperation among domestic security and intelligence services in the Gulf states.[10] The remaining Gulf states were generally sympathetic with either the Kuwaiti or Saudi positions.

The different views of the threats in the region affected the member states' predispositions toward cooperating with the superpowers. Oman in this early period was concerned with Soviet activities on and around the Arabian Peninsula; the Omanis reportedly advanced proposals to the GCC calling for full cooperation with the US and the West.[11] Kuwait, which had traditionally sought security against Iraq by its special relationship with Moscow, would not accept such a pro-American approach. The Kuwaitis argued that increased cooperation with the US would only stimulate greater Soviet activity in the Gulf.[12] The Saudis, more concerned with internal threats, agreed with the Kuwaitis on this point. Oman found no supporters for its position among the other GCC states.

When the GCC statutes were signed by the Gulf heads of state in May 1981, security was not listed as one of the fields of cooperation for which the organization was created.[13] In a separate final statement released at the end of the first GCC summit, the members established their organization's declaratory policy on military cooperation with external powers:

> Their majesties and highnesses reviewed the current situation in the area. They reaffirm that *the region's security and stability are the responsibility of its peoples* and countries and that this Council expresses the will of these countries and their right to defend their security and independence. They also affirm their absolute rejection of foreign interference in the region from any source. *They call for keeping the entire region free of international conflicts, particularly the presence of military fleets and foreign bases*, in order to safeguard their interests and the interests of the world [emphasis added].[14]

In the following years, largely in response to regional developments, the positions of the GCC states on security cooperation showed evidence of converging. By the fall of 1981 the Iraqi offensive against Iran had long since peaked, and Iran began its campaign to dislodge Iraqi forces from its territory. The Iranian offensive included an attack on Kuwaiti oil installations in October; in December 1981, an Iranian-supported plot was unveiled to overthrow the government of Bahrain and establish an Islamic republic.[15] By early 1982, with growing threats of Iranian-supported subversion in the Gulf, Saudi Arabia succeeded in signing bilateral internal security pacts with Bahrain, Qatar, the UAE and Oman.[16] Kuwait remained outside of the Saudi security network largely because it refused to agree to the expanded extradition arrangements and the rights of hot pursuit that the agreements would have granted Saudi Arabia.[17] Still unwilling to make any formal arrangements governing internal security threats, Kuwait did, however, indicate a new willingness to see the GCC coordinate on issues of external security. This was especially so after mid-1983, as the emerging stalemate in the Iran-Iraq land war threatened to bring about attempts by both parties to carry their conflict to the waters of the Persian Gulf. Oman, for its part, since the very creation of the GCC showed increasing indications that it was ready to retreat from its advocacy of firm security ties to the US. As noted in the previous chapter, the Omanis — after initially agreeing to participate in the RDJTF's *Bright Star 82*, held during late 1981 — suddenly placed unexpected restrictions on the US Marines' exercises on Omani territory. By the time *Bright Star 83* was held in late summer of 1983, Oman was no longer included on the roster of states hosting American forces. Clearly the gap between the two extremes in the GCC had narrowed.

The completion of the transformation of the GCC from a mini-Arab EEC, focusing on economic and social affairs, to a nascent military grouping occurred in the fall of 1983, when the six member states held their first joint military exercises, code-named, *Dir' al-Jazira* (or "Shield of the Peninsula"), in the desert of Abu Dhabi. These exercises, involving some 5,000 ground forces from contingents of each of the GCC states, were followed during the rest of the year by a series of bilateral air and naval exercises. The background to this increasing security coordination among the GCC states was the delivery in October 1983 of five French Super Etendard aircraft armed with Exocet anti-ship missiles to Iraq, and Iraqi threats to employ the new weaponry against Iranian oil facilities and the oil tankers they served. In anticipation of Iranian retaliatory strikes, the GCC initiated not only joint exercises; by February 1984 the GCC chiefs of staff and defense ministers undertook joint contingency planning.[18] With Iranian forces at this time poised to cut the Baghdad-Basra highway, any Kuwaiti reluctance to engage in external security discussions had completely melted away.

The Tanker War Round One — Limited GCC Military Interest in American Support Against Regional Threats

Since the beginning of its war with Iraq, Iran had threatened to close the 42-kilometer wide Straits of Hormuz. But it was not until the fall of 1983, in the aftermath of the French aircraft deliveries to Iraq noted above, that the threat was taken somewhat seriously in the West. President Reagan, pronouncing US policy in October, warned that the US would not sit back quietly if Iran attempted to carry out its threat: "I don't believe the Free World could stand by and allow anyone to close the Straits of Hormuz and the Persian Gulf to the oil traffic through those waterways."[19]

As tensions mounted in the Gulf with Iraqi threats and Iranian counter-threats to Gulf shipping, the US increased its naval presence in the Arabian Sea to include a 2,000 man Marine amphibious unit redeployed from Lebanon.[20] In the late fall CENTCOM established its forward headquarters aboard the flagship of MIDEASTFOR within the Gulf itself.

As it turned out, the threat to maritime traffic through the Straits of Hormuz did not come from Iranian mining operations — which the US Navy could have handled alone — but rather from the reciprocal air attacks both states conducted against oil tankers and cargo ships seen to be serving directly or indirectly the economic interests of the other side. In February Iraq initiated the air attacks against commercial shipping along Iran's coast, and then moved against tankers in the vicinity of Kharg Island. Iran waited until May to strike back with attacks against two Kuwaiti tankers — the *Umm Kasba* and the *Bahra* — and a Saudi tanker, the *Yanbu' Pride*, which was still in Saudi territorial waters close to the port of Ras Tanura.

The US had already sought earlier in the crisis to take steps to reassure the Gulf States of their security should the Iran-Iraq War widen. A joint State-Defense delegation in early December 1983 visited Saudi Arabia, Kuwait, Bahrain, Qatar, the UAE and Oman to discuss the possibility of US-Gulf Arab cooperation if the Iranians made good on their threat to close the Straits of Hormuz. At the same time, the US group expressed the view that Washington saw an Iranian victory on land as countering American Middle East interests.[21] In April 1984, with Iraqi air attacks on Gulf shipping under way, another US team led by Assistant Secretary of State for Near Eastern and South Asian Affairs Richard W. Murphy, and the White House Deputy Assistant for National Security Affairs Vice Admiral John M. Poindexter, toured the GCC states again. The Americans were generally interested in showing US readiness to assist the Gulf states — and even to provide them with air cover — in the event that a request was made. However, the latter would have to provide expanded facilities to US forces — including airfields, radar and warehouses. The United States, it was explained, could not respond *in time* with forces from outside the region. It preferred to operate American air power from airfields on land, rather than from carriers, because the Navy would be reluctant to bring them into range of their targets in Iran by taking them into the Persian Gulf itself where they would be exposed to land-based air threats.[22]

The Gulf states, whose recent military preparations indicated that they were no less concerned about the impending threat to their shipping, nonetheless were reluctant to deepen US involvement in the Gulf. They appeared to be content to keep the United States "over the horizon" in the Arabian Sea, despite Murphy and Poindexter's explication of the operational difficulties the US faced with such deployments.[23] The attitudes of the Gulf states were somewhat complex. Thus even the Kuwaitis, known for their critical attitude toward strategic cooperation between the GCC and the United States, by May were calling openly for greater American involvement in settling the Iran-Iraq War. The Kuwaiti oil minister, Shaykh Ali al-Sabah, even criticized American passivity.[24] Militarily, while still refusing to accept foreign bases on Kuwaiti soil, Kuwait's foreign minister, Shaykh Sabah al-Ahmad al-Jabir, retreated substantially from the declared GCC position that the defense of the Gulf was the sole responsibility of the Gulf states themselves. In May he stated that he had no objections to western intervention to safeguard oil traffic:

> First, you must know that the Gulf waters are not territorial but international, governed by international agreements. The Gulf concerns me and others because it is an artery for the countries of Europe, Asia, Japan and numerous others....I do not have the right to oppose military intervention because the Gulf is international and is not a Kuwaiti, Omani, Qatari or even Arab gulf.[25]

Thus, while calling for greater American involvement, Kuwait also appeared to be outlining clear parameters of permissible military intervention in the Gulf crisis. Of the variety of air, land, and sea-based power projection forces available to the United States, the Kuwaitis, even with their tankers under attack, preferred naval intervention, confined to the Gulf's international waters. Though not saying so in public, they were also prepared to draw on intelligence gathered by US-operated AWACS based on Saudi soil.[26] Obviously, US force planners had to compromise what was operationally desirable with what was politically permissible.

The overall GCC position on US involvement, in general, was by now not far different from that of Kuwait. In June, the GCC states undertook to defend shipping against Iranian attacks within the 12-mile limit of their territorial waters.[27] This new line, referred to as the "King Fahd Line," demarcated GCC and western strategic responsibilities in the Gulf. With this territorial division of labor, the Gulf states were cautiously and in graduated fashion allowing the United States to assume a security role on their behalf.

The Gulf states' source of reluctance was three-fold. First, as Saudi Oil Minister Shaykh Ahmad Zaki Yamani noted in May, there was concern over superpower escalation: "no one will invite the US to come (to the Gulf) without thinking of the possibility of the Soviet Union also coming there."[28] Secondly, many of the Gulf states were concerned about the domestic implications of visible joint military preparations with the United States. After successive terrorist attacks on US Marine Headquarters in Beirut in October 1983 and on the US Embassy in Kuwait the following December, the states anticipated that they would only create new targets for Syrian and Iranian-sponsored terrorism.[29] Third, in the specific time-frame involved, US credibility after the decision to leave Lebanon was low. The US Marines' "redeployment" from Beirut to the Sixth Fleet was completed in February 1984, just as Iraq opened the Tanker War in the Gulf. Without judging the merits of America's original involvement in Lebanon, the departure did not leave a strong impression in the Gulf region. An unidentified GCC delegate was quoted at the time as having learned the lessons of the Lebanon affair as follows: "Frankly, we hope the Americans do not act in the Gulf. For the worst thing would be for them to intervene and not finish the job. That would leave us with a far bigger mess."[30]

Ultimately, the Gulf states were not forced to make hard choices between the dangers of increased American involvement and the dangers of going it alone. Saudi Arabia restored some confidence to the GCC when on June 5 a Royal Saudi Air Force F-15 downed an attacking Iranian F-4 Phantom. In retrospect, this first phase of the Tanker War — attacks on commercial shipping continued in subsequent years — was not particularly detrimental. It did not shut down tanker traffic through the Straits of Hormuz. Most damage to ships was light. Oil prices and availability were not affected, as the world was in the midst of an oil glut. With the wisdom of retrospect, no serious US military intervention seems to have been necessary.

Yet this kind of desirable outcome was by no means inevitable at the time. Had the Iranian Phantom downed the Saudi F-15, it is not so clear whether the Royal Saudi Air Force would have continued to scramble aircraft in pursuit of Iranian intruders. Had Iranian strategy dictated a broadening of the war in order to terminate Saudi and Kuwaiti aid to Iraq, Iran might have decided to attack Saudi oil terminals, despite the loss of one aircraft. What is significant for this analysis is that the US was not in a good position to deter, much less defend against, more negative contingencies that could just as easily have occurred.

The Tanker War Round Two — Cautious US-GCC Cooperation Against Regional Threats

During 1985 the continuing tanker attacks in the Persian Gulf were still an insufficient cause for any fundamental change in the US-GCC security relationship. The total number of Iranian attacks against tankers serving Gulf Arab ports for the entire year reached only 11; in comparison, 16 tankers had been struck by the Iranians in 1984 in the period from May to December alone.[31] Concern was instead focused on two other developments connected with the Iran-Iraq War. First, Iranian troop concentrations during the year, and the March 1985 Iranian assault in the Huwaiza marshes, threatened to cut off southern Iraq and its principal city, Basra, from Baghdad to the north. While the Iranian offensive was repulsed in an Iraqi counterattack, the GCC states — and above all Kuwait — had to address the prospect of a new revolutionary Islamic republic emerging in southern Iraq adjacent to their northern border.

Secondly, Kuwait particularly was confronted with an intensification of the frequency and lethality of terrorist attacks. These, by virtue of their connection to Kuwait's foreign Shi'ite communities, appeared to have had Iranian organizational direction or at least inspiration. Among the targets of these attempted pro-Iranian attacks were the editor of one of Kuwait's most noted newspapers, *al-Siyasa*; seaside resort cafes frequented by the shaykdom's internal security personnel; and, above all, Kuwait's ruler, Shaykh Jabir al-Sabah. In this environment of a feared Iraqi collapse and increased internal subversion, there was little the United States could do for its Gulf partners. Reportedly during the year Secretary of State George Shultz secretly pledged US aid in the defense of the territorial integrity of the GCC states in the event that they made a public request and offered military facilities.[32] As was the case with the 1984 Murphy-Poindexter mission, neither of these preconditions was met in 1985. Nevertheless, Washington appeared to have recognized not only the need to make preparations in response to the tanker war, but also the prospect of a future expanded land war encompassing its Gulf partners as well.

Events in 1986 pushed Kuwait far ahead of its GCC neighbors in seeking a more activist approach from the United States in the Gulf region. At the start of the year, Iran seemed again about to break the stalemate in the ground war with its successful offensive into the Faw Peninsula at the southern tip of Iraq. Pressure immediately built up on Kuwait over whether it had — or would soon — let the Iraqis use its strategically located islands of Bubiyan and Warbah directly across from Iranian-held Faw. Iranian suspicions of Kuwait and other Gulf states during the year were further intensified after the Iraqi Air Force successfully conducted long-range bombing attacks against Iran's remote Sirri and Larak island oil terminals in the lower Gulf. GCC collaboration in providing ground facilities to the Iraqi aircraft seemed to the Iranians to be far more likely than an Iraqi mid-air refueling capability.

In the tanker war itself, newly deployed Iranian equipment and altered tactics promised now to threaten all shipping serving Gulf Arab ports. Iran took possession of its first Chinese-made HY-2 Silkworm anti-ship missile batteries in the summer of 1986; the Silkworm system substantially increased the limited anti-ship threat previously emanating from the tiny Iranian Air Force. At the same time, Iran increased its effectiveness in the Gulf by making greater use of its navy. Iranian warships for the first time began to stop and search freighters of all nations — including those of the

US, USSR, and Britain — suspected of carrying weapons bound for Iraq via Gulf ports. Not surprisingly, the number of tankers attacked by Iran in 1986 tripled in comparison with 1985 (38 against the 11 noted above).[33] With the scope and intensity of Iranian operations in the waters of the Gulf greatly expanded, and with several Gulf states — above all, Kuwait — repeatedly accused by Tehran of proffering not just financial but also operational military support to Iraq, the GCC's aloof attitude to security collaboration with the US underwent serious reexamination.

The formal occasion for an updated evaluation of GCC security policy was the annual GCC summit meeting, held in November 1986 in Abu Dhabi. At that time Kuwait reportedly sought GCC approval for a new strategy of superpower protection of Gulf shipping. The Gulf leaders did not receive the Kuwaiti offer enthusiastically; both Oman and the UAE were still loath to alienate Iran entirely by bringing in outside powers.[34] No announced change in GCC security policy emerged from the discussion at the November summit; at the same time, the other GCC states did not oppose Kuwait's unilateral efforts to safeguard its interests by turning to the superpowers. The acquiescence of the GCC probably came about because the new Kuwaiti approach essentially did not contradict past principles in the GCC security strategy. First, Kuwait did not seek to establish a superpower military presence on its territory in order to deter Iranian ground forces; it only sought to protect its tanker traffic in international waters that were beyond the "King Fahd Line" — and hence beyond the GCC's declared area of responsibility as well as capability. Secondly, by initially turning to *both* superpowers, Kuwait was preempting criticism that it was converting the Gulf region into an arena of superpower competition; had Kuwait turned to the United States alone, there would have been concern lest the Soviet Union feel compelled to counter the Kuwaiti move in some way.

Kuwait thus began to work along parallel lines with the US and the USSR. In mid-January 1987 the Kuwait government formally turned to the US Embassy to inquire whether Kuwaiti vessels reflagged as American ships would receive the same protection as US-flag vessels. Apparently, Kuwait planned to reflag 11 of its 22 tankers: five tankers under the Soviet flag and six under the US flag. On March 7 the United States, having learned the previous month of the plan to introduce Soviet-flag tankers as well, counter-offered to reflag the entire group of 11 Kuwaiti tankers. Kuwait accepted the American proposal; nevertheless, it sought to reinforce its reflagged tanker fleet by chartering three Soviet tankers.[35] Thus the principled approach to *both* superpowers had been preserved, with the Soviet Union's relative role in tanker protection operations severely reduced in magnitude.

Conceivably, neither American nor Kuwaiti officials ever anticipated that the reflagging and convoy operations they agreed to in March would result in the enormous naval buildup in the region that was well underway by late summer. After all, there was nothing new about the deployment of US naval forces within the Gulf itself; USMIDEASTFOR had been there since 1949, and its force of four to five destroyers and frigates had already undertaken considerable convoy duties of US-flag ships during 1986, in the aftermath of Iranian search and seizure operations against commercial ships serving Gulf Arab ports. On January 12, 1986, the first American-flag cargo ship, the *President Tyler*, had been stopped by the Iranians; a second US vessel, the *Ingenious* was stopped on April 25. In that sense the reflagging operation entailed the addition of Kuwaiti reflagged tankers to a mission that the US had already been involved in for at least a year. In fact in a statement before Congress in June, Secretary of Defense Weinberger claimed that the Navy's escorting of the additional Kuwaiti tankers would essentially entail augmenting MIDEASTFOR's five ships with but three additional combat vessels.[36]

Events soon demonstrated that the US needed to expand its military presence in the Gulf region significantly — certainly at sea and possibly on land as well. First, the accidental attack by Iraqi Mirage aircraft on the MIDEASTFOR frigate, the *USS Stark*, that caused the death of 37 American sailors, underlined the vulnerability of the American naval presence to coastal air attack. US air cover was clearly needed over the Gulf's international waters, as the mission of friendly Saudi air superiority aircraft was confined to the defense of Saudi airspace alone. It had been for this reason, American officials later explained, that Saudi F-15s did not pursue and intercept the Iraqi Mirage.[37] The need to provide improved air cover for the American naval convoys increased the importance of maintaining a year-round carrier presence in the Arabian Sea — not just for seven months a year. Similarly, by virtue of the fact that American carriers would not enter the Gulf itself — exposing themselves to hostile air or missile attack — ground support facilities for American naval airpower became an increasingly desirable element in enhancing US air cover over convoy operations; GCC air bases could provide landing and refueling flights for naval fighters operating at the limits of their range, especially in the Upper Gulf.

Yet even with the United States fully involved in the protection of Kuwait's oil tanker trade, clearcut GCC base support for US air cover operations was not always provided. In June Secretary Weinberger was hard put to describe the ways in which the Saudis were providing allied support for the enlarged US presence.[38] He claimed that Royal Saudi Air Force fighters provided protection for the US Air Force's Saudi-based AWACS that were deployed in the kingdom since 1980. The US AWACS, he added, gave early warning protection to MIDEASTFOR, thereby implying a Saudi role in assisting the US naval convoy mission. The US AWACS, he noted, only operated in Saudi airspace. Given that it was the regular mission of the Royal Saudi Air Force to protect the kingdom's airspace, in any case — with or without the US AWACS — then the Saudis had not really gone out of their way to help US forces. To claim that the Saudis provided allied support by protecting the US AWACS was thus somewhat misleading. To Saudi Arabia's credit however, it appears that after the Iranian-sponsored violence in Mecca in July, Riyadh softened its reluctance to assist US forces in the Gulf. The Saudis were reportedly ready to provide fighter cover for US AWACS operating outside of Saudi airspace in the Lower Gulf. Some US carrier-based aircraft may have begun to receive logistics support on a case-by-case basis. But no change was apparent regarding the routine basing of US fighter planes.[39]

The first convoy of US reflagged Kuwaiti tankers got underway on July 22; the tanker *Bridgeton* was holed by an Iranian mine two days later. It immediately became apparent to US military authorities that the anti-mine-warfare capabilities of MIDEASTFOR and its supporting forces would have to be expanded far more than previously thought. As early as May 16 a Soviet tanker, the *Marshal Chuykov*, had struck an Iranian mine off Kuwait, and further mines were discovered by US forces on July 1 in the same area, but neither of these incidents had altered the American decision to begin convoy operations without adequate minesweeping equipment. Basing US Navy minehunting Sea-Stallion helicopters in Kuwait would promptly have expanded US anti-mine capabilities in the area where initially most of the mines were discovered. The Sea-Stallions were airlifted to the Gulf region and could have been deployed quickly. But Kuwait's apparent reluctance to see its territories used by foreign combat forces delayed the full introduction of anti-mine procedures. Only in the first week of August, with the arrival of the amphibious assault ship the *USS Guadalcanal*, did the Navy's Sea-Stallions acquire a platform for operations against Iranian mines. Thus the second American convoy only began to move on August 8. Subsequently MIDEASTFOR reportedly set up its own temporary "floating base," built on a platform straddling two barges anchored some 12 miles from Bahrain harbor.[40] As for Kuwait, it principally assisted US forces in the Gulf by acting as one of their fuel suppliers; Kuwait sold fuel on a commercial basis to the entire US task force and offered to pay for the fuel needed by MIDEASTFOR during its escort operations.[41]

The pattern established with regard to US-GCC state strategic interaction in a regional contingency scenario during the Tanker War crisis may be summarized as follows. The GCC states showed an obvious readiness — under stress — to abandon their principal objection to American military involvement in Gulf security. But by no means were they willing to do so entirely, and even under stressful conditions they preferred to keep US forces off their sovereign territories. While normally preferring to keep their American protectors in the Arabian Sea "over the horizon," under crisis conditions they were prepared to see the horizon come close to their shores.

During the reflagging and convoy operations of 1987, the horizon had approached GCC territorial waters; US strategic responsibilities began in the Gulf's international waters. Iran's strategy appeared to take this distinction into account in September and October when its Silkworm missile batteries, deployed in the Faw Peninsula, repeatedly targeted Kuwait's ports and oil terminal. Attacked beyond the American umbrella, Kuwait was placed in a clear dilemma: either extend American protection to Kuwaiti territory — with all its possibly destabilizing domestic effects — or terminate the reflagging arrangements and accept Iranian hegemony. Kuwait first appeared to try a third course of marshalling diplomatic and economic counterpressures on Iran through the GCC and the Arab summit. By December, however, the embattled Kuwaitis seemed ready to make another incremental concession to their American protectors: a US request to set up another "floating-base" *within* Kuwaiti territorial waters was approved.[42] Only after repeated Iranian missile strikes did Kuwait cautiously modify its security policy.

Political and strategic constraints thus placed limitations on American-GCC military cooperation in regional crises. In a way both constraints were linked and formed a vicious circle. If US officials argued that certain land-based deployments were necessary for protecting the Gulf and that otherwise American capabilities were limited, then local officials might wonder whether it was worthwhile depending on US protection. Facing dangerous dilemmas in openly striking common cause with the US, the Gulf states might elect in a future crisis to pursue a policy of accommodation rather than confrontation backed by American strength. Under these conditions, coalition-building for CENTCOM — and the formation of some kind of political-military consensus with the GCC for contingency planning in regional crises around the oil-producing areas — will probably remain an extremely difficult task.

The GCC and the Soviet Threat

If the establishment of a working US-Gulf state coalition in a regional threat scenario is as difficult as described above, in the case of planning against possible future Soviet threats the situation can be described as even less promising. The Gulf states, known for their Islamic conservatism, appear from an ideological perspective alone to be ideal candidates for an anti-communist coalition. Yet regional developments over the last half-decade have increased their interest in closer ties with the USSR, while reducing significantly their sense of the primary threat to their security emanating from the Soviet Union or its regional allies.

A shift in Saudi attitudes toward the USSR — from ideological rejection of the Soviet system to a pragmatic appreciation of the extent of Soviet influence — came in the period of 1977-1979 as Moscow refocused its political-military activism in the Middle East in regions immediately surrounding the Saudi kingdom.[43] Saudi receptivity to Soviet probes under these newly threatening conditions was further promoted by Riyadh's perception of American weakness as well as by its perception of Soviet strength. With the Soviet invasion of Afghanistan, for several months Saudi Arabia took diplomatic initiatives that were openly critical of the

USSR. But within a short time span the Saudis appeared to have returned to their earlier stance of seeking to maintain quiet working understandings with Moscow. Even a month after the Soviet invasion Fahd, in his capacity as Crown Prince, chose to minimize the Saudi role as the West's anti-Soviet surrogate in the Arab world. He frankly confessed: "in the circumstances we cannot but admit that the Soviet Union is a major power and that we want no problems with it."[44]

These cautious attitudes toward the USSR were expressed when Saudi Arabia experienced Soviet encirclement either by means of Soviet regional allies (Ethiopia, Iraq, PDRY) or by means of more direct Soviet pressures (the invasion of Afghanistan). The rise of revolutionary Iran and the outbreak of the Iran-Iraq War led to the eclipse of the threat from the Left and the emergence of a new threat from the religious Right. In the past, a large part of Saudi concern over Soviet policies had emanated from the support Moscow gave to revolutionary regimes hostile to the continuation of Saudi monarchial rule. Now the Soviets, as much as they might have aspired to exercise influence in the new Iran, could not be linked to Iranian excesses. Despite their attempted flirtations with Tehran, the Soviets remained Iraq's principal military backer. As successive Islamic and non-aligned intermediaries failed to persuade Iran to cease its offensive campaign against Iraq, Saudi Arabia and its Gulf allies became interested in preserving good relations with any power capable of bringing pressure to bear on Tehran. Soviet officials for their part openly warned Iran against taking any action that would precipitate foreign intervention.[45] Thus Saudi-Soviet interests that had so diverged at the end of the 1970s now seemed to overlap considerably, largely as a by-product of the Iran-Iraq War.

These shifts were only evident in certain nuances of Saudi-Soviet relations, such as increased bilateral trade and visits of high-level Saudi officials to Moscow. But in the other GCC states far more noticeable shifts in policy toward the USSR have been evident. This is especially true in Oman — the only GCC state to have granted the US access to its facilities. With the Dhufari insurgency under control despite the Iranian military withdrawal from Oman, the Omanis have become less concerned about the dangers of PDRY-supported subversive operations in the sultanate. Kuwaiti diplomatic initiatives in the early 1980s, aimed at reducing Omani dependence on the United States, sought to bring about a dialogue between Oman and its pro-Soviet peninsular rival, PDRY. On October 27, 1982, representatives of both countries signed a joint declaration of principles by which they agreed to bring to an end their regional political rivalry. Since then the two parties have not progressed with the normalization of relations as was originally expected — ambassadors were not exchanged and talks on the demarcation of their mutual border have stalled. Nonetheless, by the fall of 1983 Oman's ruler, Sultan Qabus expressed his satisfaction with PDRY's adherence to the principle of non-interference in his country's internal affairs.[46] Moreover, PDRY's reported force deployments at the time — three brigades against Oman and nine brigades against the Yemen Arab Republic — gave further indication that Oman was not PDRY's top security priority.[47] Since the emergence of a new government in PDRY following the January 1986 intra-party civil conflict, the Omani-PDRY dialogue has been resumed.[48]

The upshot of these developments for Soviet-Omani relations was generally positive. Qabus explained his country's refusal to establish diplomatic relations with the USSR in 1983 by stating that Oman would not have relations with any power that interfered in its internal affairs.[49] Surprisingly, on September 26, 1985, Oman and the Soviet Union announced that they would shortly be establishing diplomatic relations. Judging by previous Omani declarations, some Soviet undertaking may have been given concerning a cessation of support for anti-Omani organizations — such as the Popular Front for the Liberation of Oman (PFLO) — either directly or indirectly through the PDRY. In any case we have noted that, even without such an explicit Soviet undertaking, PDRY-supported threats to Oman had declined as a result of regional diplomatic initiatives. Whatever privately transpired between Soviet and Omani representatives, Soviet leverage over PDRY and the new Soviet-Omani diplomatic link had become a new factor in Oman's security, along with Oman's military link with the US and CENTCOM. While the former brought Oman's foreign policy into line with the GCC's non-aligned declaratory policies, the latter, to the extent it became public, isolated Oman within the organization.

On the face of it, the broadening of Oman's diplomatic ties with the USSR should not have had any necessary impact on US-Omani relations. Washington never made an exclusive claim on Muscat's external affairs. Yet Omani willingness in 1980 to reach facilities-access agreements with the United States was based on mutual Omani-American perceptions of the Soviet threat to Southwest Asia. The new Omani assessment of the reduced urgency of the Soviet threat could only weaken Sultan Qabus' resolve to cooperate with the US on the basis of anticipated anti-Soviet scenarios. This already became apparent in mid-1985 when Omani-Soviet contacts were well underway. At this time, the United States and Oman entered into discussions for the purpose of renegotiating the original 1980 facilities agreement. Washington reportedly was interested in expanding the original arrangement to include greater servicing of naval ships as well as increased prepositioning of American equipment. Qabus reportedly opposed any further expansion of the American presence, and signaled that its future prospects could not be taken for granted:

> We will never accept these bases. Our Washington friends know this well and are perfectly aware of the nature of the military facilities which we have granted them as was stipulated in the agreement signed in 1980, which will remain in force until 1990. *We have no intention of amending it, still less of extending it*[50] [emphasis added].

Beyond Oman, the USSR and the UAE announced their agreement to establish diplomatic relations on November 13, 1985. The UAE decision was not so much a function of any change in the Federation's threat-environment as it was an expression of its desire to affirm its non-aligned status; moreover, in light of the fact that a year earlier the UAE had established diplomatic relations with the People's Republic of China, the newer tie to Moscow balanced the earlier tie to Peking.[51] Of possible greater importance for the United States was the significance of the UAE decision for assessing Saudi attitudes, as it is highly unlikely that Shaykh Zayid ibn Sultan al-Nuhayan, the UAE president and ruler of Abu Dhabi, would take such an initiative without a green light from Riyadh.[52] Bahrain, which hosts MIDEASTFOR's Administrative Support Unit, still did not maintain diplomatic relations with Moscow, but nonetheless gave some indications that it may be the next Gulf state to do so. In mid-1985 Prime Minister Shaykh Khalifa ibn Salman al-Khaliya expressed the Bahraini view as follows:

> At present, we do not have relations with the Soviet Union. I think we in the Gulf must reconsider our relations with countries, especially since the Soviet Union is a superpower

like the United States....As a matter of fact a few years ago, I did not recommend the idea of establishing relations with the Soviet Union, *but now I think we must reconsider our policies*[53] [emphasis added].

The fact that three out of the six GCC states now had diplomatic relations with the USSR — Kuwait established diplomatic links with Moscow in 1963 — was not in itself a source of alarm for Washington. America's NATO allies also have diplomatic relations with the USSR. Of greater concern is whether the political motivations that have led them to this change may bring about further modifications of policy toward the United States. Soviet diplomacy vis-a-vis NATO-Europe is directed at countries already belonging to a western coalition. At best, Moscow can achieve pressures on American arms control negotiating positions or on the deployments of particular weapons systems on European soil. In the Gulf, Soviet diplomacy is aimed at a group of countries whose political coalition with the US is not yet formed. In NATO-Europe a US military presence and the equipment for its expansion are already in place for balancing Soviet conventional superiority in Eastern Europe. With regard to the Gulf, the forces and equipment needed to balance the Soviet Union's conventional ground superiority are located in surrounding seas or as far away as the continental United States; a political decision by the GCC states during a crisis is still necessary to bring them on land within striking distance of Soviet forces. The military-strategic implications of Soviet diplomatic successes are therefore more far-reaching in regions like Southwest Asia, where the successful formation of a pro-western coalition and the decision to deploy US forces have yet to be determined.

To the extent, in future years, that the USSR succeeds in diminishing any sense of a direct Soviet threat on the Gulf states — its troubles in digesting Afghanistan may be reassuring enough — and demonstrates a capability of restraining regional threats, whether from PDRY or Iran, Moscow may have a good chance of deepening its ties with the Gulf states. In order to accomplish its strategic goals, the USSR does not have to go so far as to displace the US in the Gulf. It only has to broaden the diplomatic considerations of the GCC states and nudge them — particularly Saudi Arabia and Oman — sufficiently in the direction of neutralism so as to restrict American military usage of their territories.

Outside the GCC: Alternative Partners for the Defense of Southwest Asia

Given the political limitations on a US-GCC strategic partnership, several alternative strategic partners have been groomed by the US in the regions flanking the Arabian Peninsula. Each of these alternative partners — Jordan, Egypt, and Pakistan — has its own substantial interests in the Gulf region and hence would be predisposed to take a more active role in Gulf security even if the United States were not in the background promoting some of these relationships. The alternative partners not only offer the possible use of their territories in high intensity contingencies involving the USSR, but also offer the possible use of their military manpower in more limited contingencies of intra-regional conflict or internal regime threats for which the deployment of US forces would be highly controversial.

Jordan

Jordanian involvement in CENTCOM's mission is best known in connection with reports in the fall of 1983 that for the previous two and a half years the United States had been training a Jordanian strike force for military emergencies in the Persian Gulf. This Jordanian rapid deployment force was reported to have consisted of two brigades, each comprising 4,000 troops. The force and its equipment were to be airlifted to trouble spots in the Gulf arena, according to plans, by both Jordanian and US transport aircraft. Four countries were specifically mentioned as possible venues for any Jordanian intervention: Bahrain, Oman, North Yemen, and Saudi Arabia. The latter seems to have been included since the force was first conceived in the aftermath of the difficulties the Saudis encountered in dealing with the militant takeover of the Grand Mosque in Mecca during 1979. The plan for the Jordanian strike force was part of the classified section of the Department of Defense's annual appropriations. In October 1983, with plans for the force revealed, Congress blocked the $225 million in secret financing planned for its equipment. Congress feared that the secret budget was nothing but a rear door for providing Jordan with military equipment whose transfer Congress was not willing to approve openly.[54]

Jordan was highly embarrassed by the disclosures regarding

the existence of the force. King Hussein denied that the Jordanian Army would fight on behalf of a major power; he did not deny, however, Jordan's willingness to come to the assistance of any Arab state requesting its help. In such cases, he explained, Jordan would act out of self-interest rather than in the service of the United States. He did admit that Jordan was seeking arms from Washington in order to help it respond more effectively to such crises in friendly states.[55]

Jordan was not known to have made any facilities available to the United States in higher intensity contingencies involving the US and the USSR. Jordanian fears of Syrian provocations and consequently Jordanian needs for friendly ties with Moscow, together serve to constrain Jordan's integration in peacetime into any American strategic system in the Middle East directed against the Soviet Union, or its interests.

Egypt

Egypt could potentially offer the United States an intervention force similar to that planned for Jordan. Only scant reports have mentioned that such a force is even under consideration.[56] As reported in Chapter 3, Egypt has emerged as the key for US CENTCOM strategies in the region, despite its distance from Iran. A friendly Egypt ensures shortened sea distances for resupply of US forces from either the east coast of the continental US or from Western Europe through the Suez Canal to the Arabian Peninsula. Were the Canal to be closed to the US in wartime, the Soviets would acquire a distinct advantage in the rapid deployment race to the Gulf. Egyptian airfields like Qena and Cairo West that have been used by the US Air Force in the past could well serve as rear staging areas — beyond the range of Soviet tactical theater aircraft — for US forces operating in the Arabian Peninsula or in Iran. Egypt has been willing to give the US access to its territories in peacetime, especially in large bilateral joint maneuvers like the Bright Star series. But as we have explained, Egypt has not been willing to sign any written agreement that would formalize US military access to its facilities; for this reason US funding to modernize the remote Ras Banas base on the Red Sea was not approved by Congress.

While leading Egyptian opinion maintains a traditional dislike for anything resembling foreign bases on Egyptian soil, the current level of US-Egyptian strategic cooperation is chiefly criticized by the Egyptian opposition. Both President Mubarak and Defense Minister Abu Ghazala view the strategic relationship as a net gain for Egypt. US-Egyptian joint exercises, according to the latter, benefit the Egyptian Army more than the US military; they introduce the Egyptian soldier to the latest western military equipment. The Soviets, he points out, exercised on Egyptian soil without informing Egyptian authorities; they certainly did not conduct joint maneuvers. While in 1970 President Nasser leased the USSR a military base which was off-limits to Egyptian military personnel, Abu Ghazala points out that facilities are made available to the US for specific missions only, and never leave the host country's command or sovereign control.[57]

Egyptian-American strategic cooperation, given these sorts of considerations, has been positive on the whole, although Egypt has exhibited a degree of caution about the extent of the relationship. In a wide-ranging survey of US-Egyptian relations which appeared in the Egyptian daily *Al-Ahram* in March 1986, several points of mutual interest between the countries are noted, but points of controversy between them are also raised. For example, "The US is interested in having military bases in Egypt that will serve her anti-Soviet strategy; however, Egypt does not want to be a part of US global strategy against any side, and opposes foreign bases on her soil."[58] In this way Egypt still reveals certain sensitivities about preserving its non-aligned status. At the same time, Abu Ghazala in no way restrains his ongoing anti-Soviet views when comparing superpower policies in the Middle East in both western and Arabic periodicals:

> There exists the baseless view that the Soviet Union does not need the oil of the region, however in reality oil production is steadily dropping in the USSR...therefore the USSR is driving to take control of the oil of the Gulf, or she is trying to trap the oil inside of a ring of encirclement from the Horn of Africa to Bab al-Mandab to Afghanistan.[59]

Recent improvements in Soviet-Egyptian relations, including Moscow's grant in April 1987 of a 25-year moratorium on Cairo's three billion dollar military debt, have not yet impinged on US-Egyptian strategic ties. Having undertaken a multi-year program of reorienting its forces from Eastern Bloc to western military equipment, Egypt is unlikely to make any rapid strategic shifts back in the direction of Moscow. In lesser scenarios with the Arab world, Egypt may have problems openly coordinating with the

United States against a fellow Arab state, as evidenced by critical Egyptian responses to American air strikes on its neighboring rival, Libya. Egypt was known to have shied away from any coordinated military efforts with the US against Libya, prior to the American raid.[60]

In sum, Egypt is probably the CENTCOM region Arab state that is most ready to cooperate with the US in the latter's Middle Eastern defense strategies. That fact is reflected in the size and scale of US-Egyptian exercises throughout the 1980s. In an anti-Soviet scenario, the United States would probably have the best chances of gaining access to facilities in any Arab state within the CENTCOM AOR in Egypt. In lesser scenarios in the Gulf region, Egypt, like Jordan, may have reasons of its own for giving limited backing to its conservative Gulf allies, and these tend to dovetail with American interests. Thus, threatened Egyptian workers are represented in large numbers in Iraq and throughout all the lesser Gulf states. Moreover, the new pipelines connecting Gulf oil fields to the Red Sea have given Egypt new interest in helping to preserve the free flow of oil. Certainly Egypt's emerging role as the strategic backbone of the Arab world vis-a-vis Iran has helped to bring about a dramatic improvement in its regional diplomatic standing since 1987. In the latter part of 1987 Egypt stepped up its military presence in Kuwait, dispatching air defense technicians and even some fighter pilots. Conceivably, Egypt might even dispatch limited ground forces to the Arabian Peninsula, especially in the aftermath of the withdrawal of 10,000 Pakistani soldiers from Saudi Arabia.[61] Still, a wide gap exists between signaling commitment to the Gulf states' defense — which has clear financial and diplomatic benefits — and entering the land war on the side of Iraq. Abu Ghazala has gone on record saying that Egyptian forces would not take an active part in the Gulf war even if the balance of power tilted in Iran's favor.[62]

Pakistan

While not an Arab state, Pakistan has assumed an increasingly important role in many aspects of the security of the Gulf. A Pakistani security role in this area is not particularly new. The main source of manpower for the British Empire in its ground operations in the Gulf was the Muslim population of British India. In 1980 these traditional ties were renewed when Saudi Arabia and

Pakistan entered into talks over the stationing of Pakistani combat troops on Saudi soil.[63] By 1987 the Pakistani presence appeared to have grown to at least 10,000 soldiers, including not only engineers and support personnel but also army combat forces.[64] Pakistani troops have apparently already seen action on the Peninsula: during border clashes between Saudi Arabia and the Yemen Arab Republic in 1983, Pakistani forces were reportedly taken prisoner.[65]

Difficulties arose with the Pakistani presence in Saudi Arabia by late 1987, when it emerged that a substantial number of the Pakistani forces were Shi'ites. Apparently, Saudi Arabia was concerned about their pro-Iranian sentiments, while Pakistan was not anxious to see its soldiers embroiled in a showdown between Iran and Saudi Arabia. Thus on December 2, 1987 the Saudis announced that the military contract that governed the Pakistani presence had expired; only a smaller group of pilots and technicians would remain in the country.[66]

Besides Pakistan's possibly active role in lesser military contingencies in the Gulf, Pakistan itself is ideally situated for assisting the United States in any major contingency involving Soviet intervention in Iran. The Pakistani port of Gwadar near the Iranian border is as close to the Straits of Hormuz as the Omani island of Masira. US sea-based equipment in the Indian Ocean unloaded in Pakistan would be close to a variety of possible areas of operations around the Gulf. Currently, Gwadar is little more than a fishing village; none of the facilities development funds associated with the RDF or CENTCOM were directed toward Pakistani facilities. As a result, port facilities and infrastructure throughout the general area of Pakistani Baluchistan, bordering on Iran, are relatively primitive. The US Agency for International Development has initiated a road-building project in Baluchistan that might lead to more suitable conditions for eventually developing US-funded facilities in the future.[67]

As in previously cited cases, a number of factors constrain US-Pakistani cooperation over Gulf security. US-Pakistani relations, generally, must deal with the conflict between the Pakistani nuclear program and US non-proliferation policy. Because of Pakistan's critical importance as a conduit to Afghanistan, the US Congress has attempted to reach a new understanding with the Pakistanis in this sensitive area. With regard to cooperation on Gulf security, in particular, the idea of a foreign military presence on Pakistani soil is hardly more acceptable to the Pakistani public than to the publics of neighboring Arab states. Pakistani opposition elements, including Benazir Bhutto, have criticized the government of General Zia ul-Haq for not being candid about the nature of concessions to the United States.[68] These accusations led to an explicit denial by Foreign Minister Sahabzada Yaqub Khan regarding the existence of American facilities.[69] A further limitation on coordination derives from changing threat scenarios in the Gulf. Pakistan may feel more threatened by the USSR than other possible American regional partners, but in non-Soviet scenarios, US-Pakistani understanding may be more limited. This has been evident recently regarding Pakistani policy of tilting toward Iran, as already alluded to, partly out of consideration for Pakistan's own substantial 15 percent Shi'ite minority.[70]

GCC Reactions to Non-GCC Regional Intervention

In any major confrontation between the US and the USSR in Iran or elsewhere in Southwest Asia, the GCC states would probably not be concerned with American basing preferences outside of the Arabian Peninsula. However, in smaller intraregional conflict scenarios the GCC states collectively and individually have been known to voice strong opinions over who precisely should defend the oil fields of the Persian Gulf. Speaking for the Gulf states as a group, GCC Secretary-General Abdallah Bishara explained in late 1983 that a Jordanian intervention force for the Gulf was not consistent with his organization's strategy: "We appreciate Jordan's concern over this, but it is not in line with our policy."[71] Bishara's statement was consistent with that of the GCC's most powerful member, Saudi Arabia, which in mid-1984 reportedly informed Amman that it disapproved of Jordanian intervention schemes.[72]

Not all the GCC states have argued individually with Saudi policy on this point. Bahrain's Foreign Minister Shaykh Muhammad Ibn Mubarak al-Khalifa asserted in mid-1984: "Everyone must know [that] we are not embarrassed to seek help of Jordanian or [other] Arab forces."[73] Kuwait, with memories of the positive role played by an Arab League joint force in 1961 during its first border crisis with Iraq, continues to place a premium on its defense ties with Arab states outside of the GCC. As noted earlier, during 1987 Kuwait became increasingly receptive to the dispatch of Egyptian air defense technicians and pilots, as the Iranian threat looked more menacing. Oman, which received Jordanian assistance in the 1970s during the Dhufar War, also has been receptive to a continuing Jordanian role in Gulf security.[74] For all of these states that have recently been pressed with external and internal security challenges, a security connection with Jordan or any other pro-western Arab state not only adds increased military capabilities to those proffered by their Saudi partners, but also serves to counterbalance their growing dependence on Saudi Arabia since the GCC was created. As of early 1988, Saudi principled objections to a large Egyptian security role in the Arabian Peninsula appeared to have softened, especially in the aftermath of the withdrawal of the Pakistani units that had served there since the early 1980s.

On the whole, regional reactions to CENTCOM strategies demonstrate that most states of the region have strong reasons why they might not choose to become integrated into an American-led strategic system despite the continuing Soviet occupation of Afghanistan. First, the direct Soviet overland threat for most of the states in the CENTCOM AOR is not the most pressing threat they face. CENTCOM's experience in the 1980s, in this sense, has not been unlike the US experience in attempting to organize the defense of the Middle East in the 1950s: while originally conceived to cope with direct Soviet threats to Southwest Asia, CENTCOM is most needed and appreciated from the regional viewpoint for its contribution to local security against more frequent intraregional threats. Secondly, these states have learned that a *positive* relationship with the Soviet Union can help neutralize or counterbalance Moscow's threatening regional partners. That has been the case not only with Kuwait since the 1960s, in developing special ties with the USSR because of Iraq; it appears to have been an important factor for Jordan as well in recent years due to anxiety about Syria's attitude, and to a lesser extent for Oman, that has traditionally had difficulties with PDRY.

In this sense Soviet penetration of the Middle East may have entered a new phase: its origins date back to the early 1960s, but it has only recently gathered momentum. Prior to this time, the Soviets either directly threatened Middle Eastern states (Iran, 1946; Afghanistan, 1979-80) or developed military patron-client relations with regionally expansionist countries. Now a third form of penetration is becoming evident; it is built on the accommodative policies of the region's weaker, conservative states, especially during periods when American credibility is low. Blocking Soviet influence in such cases entails offering local states strong American security ties instead of those that Moscow may be selling. In the Gulf in 1987 the United States precluded an expanded Soviet role by developing a range of security ties with Kuwait and the other GCC states chiefly through Saudi Arabia.

The GCC states, by virtue of the fact that they control the resources that make this region so important to US interests, are the ideal partners for any American security structure. But as regional sensitivities have limited American coordination with the GCC states, several alternative American partners have been developed that individually have interests in Gulf security. US policy has appreciated their potential contributions, but ought to consider as well the rivalries that exist even among friendly states in the area. Thus while full-scale Hashemite-Saudi rivalries in the Arabian Peninsula ended in 1925, memories of the Egyptian drive for hegemony in the area from the early 1960s may not have entirely dissipated. Pakistan has an unrivaled presence in the Gulf region that does not appear to have aroused any controversy among the GCC states. Moreover Pakistan, which faces the Soviet threat more directly than any state in the CENTCOM AOR, should be more willing than others to develop facilities for use by US forces in major contingencies involving the USSR. But even in the Pakistani case, local political sensitivities dictate low-profile security ties with the United States.

Under these conditions US strategy would be served by maximizing the number of possible alternative strategic partners for CENTCOM in the Middle East. Whether Israel might contribute to US security interests in this regard is the subject of the following chapter.

5. Israel and CENTCOM

Since the United States was first drawn into planning for the security of the postwar Middle East, Washington has had to reconcile at least two of its prominent interests in the region: the defense of western strategic interests from direct or indirect Soviet encroachments, and the security of the State of Israel. The formula selected in the 1950s for pursuing these two interests while preventing policies designed for each from clashing with one another, was to exclude Israel from western defense schemes. It was hoped that after an Arab-Israel settlement, Israeli forces might also become integrated into western defense planning. As early as 1952, Chairman of the Joint Chiefs of Staff Omar Bradley recognized Israel's possible contribution to the defense of the West. Looking three years into the future, he estimated that of the 19 ground divisions the US assessed the West needed for Middle East defense, two could be raised from Israel. Further, by 1955 only three states were expected to be able to provide the West air power in Middle Eastern defense: the UK (465 aircraft), Turkey (75 aircraft) and Israel (80 aircraft).[1] But when these purely military assessments were mixed with political-diplomatic considerations, it was recognized that it was more important first to develop cooperative military relationships with Egypt and later Iraq, and not to let Israeli involvement in western strategy alienate these possible Arab military partners.

When American military planners returned to the Middle East in 1979-80 to search for military facilities and devise a predominantly American defense strategy for the region, they were apparently moved by considerations similar to those that had guided their predecessors 30 years earlier — despite the fundamental differences between western aims in each period: in the 1950s the United States had hoped to build a coalition of western and Middle Eastern combat forces; in the 1980s the US was primarily interested in territorial access for its own combat forces. Thus in the search for facilities access agreements in 1979-80, Israel was skipped over. When the RDJTF began to conduct its large Middle Eastern exercises, none of its constituent forces ever touched Israeli soil. By the time the RDJTF evolved into CENTCOM in 1983 and its AOR was established, Israel noticeably remained under EUCOM's jurisdiction. The mission to defend the Gulf and its resources from further Soviet adventurism did not appear to take Israel into account.

US officials, looking back on the series of decisions that left Israel out of the regional infrastructure that supported rapid deployment missions, point to several understandable factors that influenced US considerations in the 1980s.[2]

— The inclusion of Israel in rapid deployment plans would place an extra burden on US attempts to secure facilities in the Arab world; it was hard enough to "sell" any American presence in these countries, let alone an American presence associated with Israel.

— Israel had a longstanding relationship with EUCOM that was responsible for past resupply missions in 1973 and would be responsible for any resupply efforts in a future war.

— Strategic planners designate theaters according to naval access. Israel as a Mediterranean country belongs in EUCOM, whereas Southwest Asia and the Gulf are an extension of the Indian Ocean and therefore belong to a separate theater. Egypt is also a Mediterranean country, but by virtue of its location along the Red Sea, it belongs to the Indian Ocean area as well.

— Inclusion of Israel in the RDJTF/CENTCOM area would complicate regional exercises as many states would refuse landing permission to US aircraft that had taken off from Israeli soil.

— CENTCOM is the American military's emissary to the Arab world.

— If the EUCOM/CENTCOM AOR border is ever adjusted, this will only happen when the degree of conflict or animosity between Israel and its neighbors is lower. We have not yet reached that point in time.

Two essential sets of issues arise from these considerations. First, by purely strategic criteria, should Israel have anything to do with defense plans for the Gulf? Secondly, to what degree would Arab states be willing to accept a strategic role for Israel in American defense planning in Southwest Asia, and must progress in the peace process precede assignment of that role to Israel?

These two issues became a matter of some public debate in the 1980s. At one end of the policy spectrum was former Department of Defense analyst and *Armed Forces Journal* editor Anthony

Cordesman, whose mammoth volume *The Gulf and the Search for Strategic Stability* attempts to integrate US defense policies toward the Gulf area and the Arab-Israel conflict. Cordesman pulls no punches when he plainly states: "The most immediate source of division within the West, and between the West and the Gulf states, is Israel."[3] The American relationship with Israel, he explains, "threatens any Gulf state that allies itself to the US." He states that Israeli policy blocks the formation of a solid western security system in the Gulf itself: "[the US] cannot hope to unite the Gulf around a stable political, military, and economic relationship with the West, or persuade it to react to the Soviet Bloc threat if the US is perceived as favoring Israel" in ways that accorded with Israeli policies in the early 1980s.[4] What is Cordesman's solution? The US, he answers, will never be able to "deal freely" with the Gulf states "unless an Arab-Israeli peace can be reached on terms acceptable to all parties involved including the Palestinians." In short, for Cordesman, a peace settlement is a prerequisite for an effective US Gulf strategy: "there can be no 'strategic consensus' without resolving the Palestinian issue."[5]

On the opposite side of the policy spectrum in Washington are the strategic analysts working for the American Israel Public Affairs Committee (AIPAC). The "AIPAC Papers on US-Israel Relations" illustrate ways in which Israel can contribute to American regional security interests. Steven J. Rosen's *The Strategic Value of Israel* does not directly discuss whether peace must precede greater employment of Israeli resources in Southwest Asia scenarios. It does raise important objective facts relating to the strategic utility of Israel in a major anti-Soviet contingency requiring large ground force deployments in the Gulf area. Two solid advantages stand out:

— Prepositioning US equipment in Israel belonging to the US Army's heavier mechanized units could substantially save the costs and deployment times required to move that equipment rapidly by air to the upper Gulf, from the US or from most other access points except for Egypt (Ras Banas) and Oman (Masira).
— Israeli prepositioning, unlike prepositioning in Oman and Upper Egypt, gives the US greater flexibility for moving the same US equipment as a "swing force" to Europe should war break out in the NATO region and not in the Gulf.

Rosen recognizes that prepositioning US equipment in Israel may entail some political costs with certain Arab states, but he asserts that "these costs are containable if handled firmly."[6] Clearly, unlike Cordesman, in Rosen's formulation diplomatic progress in Arab-Israel negotiations is not a precondition for greater US-Israel strategic cooperation. Moreover, by prepositioning equipment in Israel, according to Rosen, the US would not just be "spreading the risks" as with its arrangement with several Arab countries, but rather would be investing in the most advanced, politically stable and reliable society in the area. Israel, in this analysis, is thus not just another access point; it is the best access point.

A third approach to US-Israel cooperation regarding the political-military problems of Southwest Asia is implied in the concept of "strategic consensus" which is usually associated with the first secretary of state of the Reagan administration, Alexander Haig. Whether Haig voiced a view about the specific integration of Israel in the RDJTF/CENTCOM mission is not known. But he did recognize that friends of the United States in the Arab world and Israel faced an array of common threats, and he sought to deepen US security ties with both sides simultaneously. Progress on Arab-Israel peace and above all a solution to the Palestinian issue were not, according to Haig, a precondition for Israel to be included in a "consensus" including Egypt, Saudi Arabia, and Jordan: "The tendency to focus on the Palestinian issue distracted the West from consideration of the fact that many Middle East conflicts, and especially those around the Gulf, had little to do with Israel and could not be solved by Israeli concessions."[7]

According to Haig, US ties to the conservative regimes of the Gulf largely depended on the supply of sophisticated weaponry. America needed, in his view, to reinforce those ties with arms sales while at the same time it built up its relationship with Israel. Implicit in this view was the assumption that to deepen US-Gulf Arab ties by such sales would serve as a moderating factor in Gulf Arab attitudes to the Arab-Israel conflict.

Before turning to this highly controversial issue of whether US ties with Israel complicate American defense strategies in the Gulf — hence, how such considerations should affect Israel's inclusion in the CENTCOM AOR — a far more fundamental issue needs to be explored: whether Israel geostrategically has more to do with the Southwest Asia region or with the areas under the jurisdiction of the European command. In other words, by purely strategic criteria alone, where does Israel belong: in CENTCOM or EUCOM? The answer to this question requires an analysis of the basis of US-Israel strategic cooperation: is Israel a more useful strategic partner to the US in European scenarios or in Middle Eastern scenarios?

Israel Between EUCOM and CENTCOM

In an essay scoffing at the very idea of US-Israel strategic cooperation, Harry Shaw, a former official of the Office of Management and Budget, noted that Israeli analysts regard as "far-fetched" the notion that Israeli divisions would advance beyond Israel's borders to meet a Soviet threat toward the Persian Gulf.[8] Shaw's analysis of strategic cooperation is in some ways flawed, as he searches for cases beyond the mutual interests of both the US and Israel and attempts to show the limits of Israel's utility as a military ally. All alliances and coalitions are based on common interests; areas where interests do not overlap cannot be expected to be included in strategic cooperation. In World War II, the US and Britain found common cause against the Axis powers, but Americans were not going to die to save the British Empire. A critique of any alliance can only be useful if it is directed at the degree of assistance two states are willing to offer one another when they share a *mutual threat*. Moreover, such a critique must make distinctions between types of assistance states may be willing to offer one another. Assistance in the Middle East may range from passive measures like giving open air access, to permitting the use of sovereign facilities, to the commitment of combat forces.

Shaw's analysis is relevant, however, in relating to the problem of identifying the mutual threat that both Israel and the United States face. For the US and its NATO allies the mutual threat is more or less clear cut: it is the USSR and its Warsaw Pact allies. In the Middle East the threats to the US and Israel are different. The United States is not locked into an adversarial relationship with the Arab world. The principal threat to the Middle East from the US perspective is the USSR. At the same time, America is concerned about the activities of Soviet-supported regional states against neighboring countries friendly to the US. Furthermore, since becoming more actively engaged in the war on terrorism, the US must handle threats against its interests by independently activated regional states — such as Iran — regardless of the Soviet factor.

Israel, from its standpoint, is not locked into an adversarial relationship with the USSR; nor is it the enemy of the entire Arab world. The principal threat against Israel consists of those neighboring states, possibly including pro-western regimes, that elect to form an Arab war-coalition. In this sense Israel's perspective is similar to that of the GCC states: regional threats loom far larger than the more distant Soviet threat. At the same time, it must be added that historically Israel has been concerned about the threat of direct Soviet military intervention during an Arab-Israel war. Given these differences of orientation, where do US and Israeli security interests overlap?

Edward Luttwak has astutely observed that Israel is not a strategic asset if it helps the United States solve problems that by its existence it helped to create.[9] Thus the very fact that Israel, by defending itself adequately does not require US military intervention on its behalf cannot be counted as strategic cooperation involving a mutual interest — the continued survival of the Jewish state. Rather, the source of mutual US-Israel strategic interests can be found in a repeated dynamic of international and regional politics in the Middle East since the 1950s. The Arab world, with its independent political emergence after World War II, has undergone repeated rivalries that have been defined successively along dynastic, ideological, and military-strategic lines. Whatever the declared basis of polarization, the Arabs have roughly been divided between those states wishing to significantly *alter* the political status quo — revising the political boundaries and national identities left by the British and French — and those states seeking to *defend* the post-imperial status quo. Of course many of the principal "defenders" of the status quo maintain irredentist claims concerning their undefined borders with neighboring states, such as that of Saudi Arabia in the Buraimi Oasis, Morocco in the Western Sahara, and Pahlevi Iran in the Persian Gulf. But while each of these claims has been supported by some use of force, none has entailed the determined export of revolutionary activities aimed at both undermining the stability of neighboring rivals and installing dynastically or ideologically compatible replacements.

Since the mid-1950s states belonging to this revolutionary

anti-status quo category have had three military-strategic characteristics:

1. In order to enhance their military power sufficiently to challenge the status quo and facilitate their pursuit of regional ambitions — without significant external constraints — these states have turned to the Soviet Bloc for military assistance and support; the Soviets in turn have been strikingly receptive to these advances, so as to deepen their military-strategic penetration of the client's territory.

2. In order rightfully to claim their sought-after goal of regional or sub-regional Arab leader, these states have refused to entertain the possibility of a political settlement of the Arab-Israel conflict; on the contrary, they have sought to play the role of Arab coalition *initiators* against Israel. If geography or capabilities limited this latter aspiration, these states have at least been willing to sponsor military training and operations of Palestinian terrorist organizations against Israeli and western targets.

3. The military-strategic targets of these activist states have generally been Arab regimes closely aligned with the West. Pressures have come in the form of direct military threats, efforts at internal subversion and assassination, and support for military takeovers of the civilian government.

While the cast of characters has changed over time — Nasserist Egypt, Qaddafi's Libya, Ba'athist Iraq, and Ba'athist Syria — these traits generally came together in each case, and led to the emergence of regimes whose national policies presented mutual threats to *both* US and Israeli interests. The first case where this dynamic became apparent was in late 1962, when the Egyptian Army intervened in the Yemen Civil War on behalf of the pro-republican military forces that had overthrown the traditional Yemeni imamate. What began as a small advisory mission quickly turned into a substantial Egyptian presence on the Arabian Peninsula of some 60-70,000 troops. As Saudi Arabia and Jordan decided to support the pro-imamate forces fighting the republican government from Yemen's northern hill country, the Yemen Civil War threatened to deteriorate into a clash between Egypt and Saudi Arabia. This became particularly apparent when the Egyptian Air Force began to strike at Saudi border towns. While the United States initially attempted to mediate between Egypt and Saudi Arabia, it was eventually forced to assure the Saudis that it supported the kingdom's territorial integrity; a squadron of US Air

Force F-100 fighters was deployed in mid-1963 to Saudi Arabia for that particular purpose.[10]

Israel's role, if any, in the Yemen Civil War itself was marginal. There have been reports that Israel, like Jordan and Saudi Arabia, gave assistance to the pro-imamate forces. An Israeli scholar on Saudi Arabia has written of "continuous contacts" between Israel and Saudi Arabia during the civil war, held outside the Middle East.[11] The main contribution Israel made to the defense of Saudi Arabia apparently came as a by-product of the June 1967 War: Egypt, defeated by Israel, agreed in August 1967 to withdraw from Yemen. Until that time, none of the mediation efforts achieved Egyptian disengagement from the Arabian Peninsula. Had Egypt continued after 1967 to maintain large forces in Yemen, Egyptian influence would have undoubtedly spread to Aden with the British withdrawal the very same year. A unified Yemen supported by Egypt would have constituted an immediate threat to Saudi Arabia, to Oman, and to the lesser Gulf shaykhdoms whose political fate was very much in flux in the early 1970s.

The most famous case of the convergence of Israeli and American strategic interests was the September 1970 Jordan Civil War crisis that threatened to bring about either an Iraqi or a Syrian takeover of the Hashemite Kingdom. On September 20, 1970, three days after King Hussein ordered his army to move against the armed Palestinian presence in his kingdom, the Syrian Army invaded Jordan. Until that time US officials feared that the Iraqis might intervene on the Palestinians' behalf. Within twenty-four hours of the first Syrian tank crossing the Jordanian border, King Hussein had already requested American air strikes against the invading force. Realizing the limits of available American military forces and recognizing Israel's interest in Jordan's continued existence as a moderate neighbor, Henry Kissinger, in his capacity as assistant for national security, persuaded President Nixon and Secretary of State Rogers of the need to support an Israeli air attack against the Syrian invasion force. Later, after the Israelis concluded that air strikes against the Syrians might be insufficient and that the use of Israeli ground forces might be necessary, President Nixon approved, in principle, an Israeli ground action in Jordan subject to consultation with King Hussein.[12]

American-Israeli contingency plans did not have to be executed. It was sufficient for Washington to communicate to Moscow its concern over the crisis, move its Sixth Fleet to the Eastern

Mediterranean, and ask its Israeli partner to declare a state of mobilization. Hussein, his confidence in western backing enhanced, ultimately defeated the Syrian invasion force with Jordanian air and ground forces. The Syrians, unsure of both their Golan flank and the prospects of Soviet support, decided not to throw the full weight of their military forces against Jordan. The crisis that began on September 19 was over by September 22.

One unique quality of the Syrian-Jordanian border crisis, unlike the Egyptian intervention in Yemen, was the fact that it could be easily repeated. Between November and December 1980, the Syrians menacingly deployed two divisions along the Jordanian border on the grounds of alleged Jordanian support for the Muslim Brethren in Syria, Jordanian alignment with Iraq in its attack on Iran, and reported Jordanian support for American-sponsored peace negotiations. In this second crisis, the Syrians did not cross the Jordanian border: Arab mediation undertaken by Saudi Arabia proved sufficient to defuse the crisis and bring about a change in Syria's force deployments.

Under current command arrangements separating EUCOM from CENTCOM, the United States would have been unable to coordinate any strategic plans with Israel by means of America's unified commands in these previous incidents to Israel's east, unless the National Command Authority (the president and the secretary of defense) decided to circumvent the Unified Command System and create new ad hoc military arrangements for the Middle East. For this reason, publicly disclosed elements of regular US-Israel strategic cooperation, which has blossomed since 1983, have been focused in the EUCOM area: US Sixth Fleet port calls in Haifa, joint anti-submarine exercises, US Navy fighter training in the Negev, US use of Israeli installations, and prepositioned American equipment for crisis contingencies.[13] But by virtue of Israel's assignment to EUCOM while Jordan and Saudi Arabia are in CENTCOM, if future regional threats to Jordan or Saudi Arabia are perceived in Jerusalem as endangering Israeli national security interests as well, then US-Israel joint planning would be constrained. Operational military initiatives — ranging from Israeli mobilization to Israeli Air Force air demonstrations, to reinforcement of the threatened regime with munitions-in-theater or spare parts — could not be arranged through the US armed forces without the prior intervention of the political echelons in the technical divisions of the Unified Command Plan.

The need for such coordination is not only apparent with regard to the Syrian-Jordanian border, which could flare up again in the future, but also in connection with the Iran-Iraq War. However complex American and Israeli interests have become over the subtleties of how to "tilt" in a war involving two very undesirable regimes, both the US and Israel have a fairly clear interest in a stalemate outcome that does not allow either side to emerge victorious. Given the fact that by 1987 the chances for an Iraqi victory were practically nil, the mutual US-Israeli interest in a stalemate had increasingly become one of containing Iran. In Israel itself, this has led to reconsideration of the conventional wisdom of seeking Israeli-Iranian cooperation against the Sunni Arab states threatening Israel.[14] Should a succession of small Iranian victories eventually produce some kind of breakthrough in Iraq, both the US and Israel — as well as the rest of the Arab world — would have a clear interest in preventing the breakup of Iraq or its conversion to a puppet Islamic republic. With Israel in EUCOM and Iraq in CENTCOM, the United States and Israel have no means of militarily planning for such a scenario despite the mutual threat to their interests both states would face. Moreover, the US would not be able to take full advantage of the mutual threat perceptions held by Israel and its Sunni Arab neighbors that would result from an Iranian breakthrough. Should strategic coordination between Israel and its former rivals be sought, as in the 1970 Syria-Jordan case, it would have to result from ad hoc arrangements, probably through the National Security Council. The professional American military, aside from the Chairman of the Joint Chiefs of Staff, by virtue of his presence in the NSC, would be left out.

These limitations are particularly salient in peacetime planning or pre-war deterrence of low-scale intraregional conflicts. In actual wartime, without changing the Unified Command Plan the JCS can designate EUCOM as a "supporting command" and CENTCOM as a "supported command"; thus military assets found in the EUCOM area could come into use in CENTCOM area operations. For example, should the United States obtain permission to use US airbases in Eastern Turkey against Soviet forces in Iran, USAF units from those EUCOM bases would be flying "in support of" the CENTCOM mission. The use of Israeli bases in such a scenario would require activating the same mechanism. As "support forces" remain under the control of their original command, such support arrangements can be cumbersome and are thought by some critics to threaten the principle of the unity of command.[15] A simpler mechanism is placing out-of-area forces directly under CENTCOM's control, as is the situation for US carriers chopped to CENTCOM from PACOM's AOR in the Arabian Sea.

In sum, the placement of Israel in EUCOM raises difficult though not insurmountable problems worthy of consideration by both American and Israeli planners:

First, Israel has only a limited strategic role to play in the defense of western interests in the Arab East, especially in those cases involving intraregional conflict. An essay prepared for the 1983 Joint Chiefs of Staff Competition in the National Defense University, by a team of military and civilian experts with experience in Middle East plans, has born out this distinction clearly: "Current thinking, considering the desirability of Arab cooperation, foresees no projection of Israeli strength eastward but, rather, a contribution in the Mediterranean."[16] More recently, US Assistant Secretary of Defense Richard L. Armitage confirmed this westward orientation of US-Israel strategic cooperation: "Strategic cooperation with Israel stands on its own merits and in any case is directed primarily at the Soviet threat in the eastern Mediterranean."[17]

This does not mean that Israel has no possible role at all against anti-status quo regimes. Both Syria and Libya — two states with grandiose regional ambitions who are leaders of the rejectionist bloc — are also in the EUCOM AOR. Yet in many cases even the threats generated by these two actors reach beyond the boundaries of US-Israel cooperation in the EUCOM zone; many of the states that each of these radical regimes at times threaten (e.g., Jordan, Egypt) are in the CENTCOM AOR, which is responsible for planning for their security. Giving Israel a role in the CENTCOM AOR would broaden the parameters of US-Israeli combined planning.

A second problem arising from Israel's placement in EUCOM is connected to the EUCOM mission in Europe. With the exception of Syrian and Libyan threats to the EUCOM area specifically, the principal job of EUCOM is planning the defense of NATO-Europe. To the extent that Israel is placed in the EUCOM AOR it finds itself in an American command chiefly designed for fighting the USSR. While CENTCOM was originally conceived for blocking the Soviets in Iran, because of intraregional conflict it now finds itself engaged in handling Soviet and non-Soviet sponsored sources of instability. Keeping Israel in EUCOM in effect has the potential of pulling US-Israel cooperation in a more anti-Soviet direction — which is in theory a US interest since Washington does not want this cooperation to be perceived as "anti-Arab." The view taken here is that strategic cooperation is best exploited by both parties when it is directed against mutually perceived high-order threats. That is not to say that Israel does not oppose Soviet domination of the Eastern Mediterranean area: preventing the extension of Soviet hegemony, should Moscow decide to assert it, is obviously an Israeli interest too. Indeed, the very growth of US-Israel strategic cooperation in this vulnerable area of NATO's Southern Flank is a testimony to Israel's peception of the importance of this mission. But currently more pressing and more highly probable threats must be addressed as well. It is clearly in Washington's interest to expand its local alliance options in the Middle East in cases of intra-regional conflict. It is precisely the intra-regional threat that the US will have the most difficulty intervening against. Congressional approval of US intervention in such non-Soviet scenarios will be difficult to come by. Broadening cooperation with Israel in this area expands the range of American options in situations where the constraints on the use of American power are most effectively felt.

Two possibilities exist for remedying these problems. One is to place Israel in CENTCOM. The disadvantage of doing so stems from the impact of such a move on Israel's already fruitful relationship with EUCOM. Another possibility entails a smaller modification of the Unified Command System. Israel sits on a strategic seam that interacts with two different zones: the Eastern Mediterranean and the Persian Gulf. Turkey is in a similar position. A structure ought to exist that easily allows the United States to make use of such countries in contingencies in *both* areas. Thus, if placing Israel in the CENTCOM AOR would harm US interests in the EUCOM AOR, then *at least a mechanism should be created that gives Israel a role in CENTCOM without removing it entirely from EUCOM.* In other words, for certain contingencies, Israel should be viewed as though it is in the CENTCOM AOR, while routinely it might be kept within EUCOM. Planning this sort of flexibility for countries like Israel that sit on the border of two unified commands will become increasingly important for US forces globally as access to overseas bases and facilities dwindles in the future.

Strategic Cooperation and Arab-Israel Peace

We noted earlier the general thesis advanced by Anthony Cordesman regarding the impact of US policy toward Israel on US-Gulf strategic relations. It may be summarized as follows: an Arab-Israel peace settlement is an absolute prerequisite for the implementation of any successful US security policy in the Gulf region, let alone the formation of any "strategic consensus" that would give Israel a positive role in an American-led Middle East security structure. In essence, the implications of giving Israel a role in CENTCOM involve very similar sorts of considerations of what ought to come first: peace, or increased strategic cooperation. Cordesman's very definite answer on this score is based on two interrelated assumptions: that the American-Israeli relationship generally is the predominant factor blocking the growth of the US strategic position in the Gulf, and that it is impossible to envision Israel having any positive regional security role until a complete peace settlement is reached. Because such assumptions might guide Pentagon planners in considering whether Israel ought to be put into the CENTCOM AOR, they are analyzed below. In this section, the more general issue of whether Israel is "the cause" blocking the establishment of an American security system in the Gulf is first examined. The final section of this chapter will inquire how Israel might fit, together with several of its neighbors, into an informal kind of strategic consensus, even prior to a peace settlement.

It would be foolish to argue that the principal Gulf leaders do not really care about the Arab-Israel conflict or the Palestinian issue. Whatever their personal predilections, many states in the Arabian Peninsula, for example, have substantial Palestinian emigrant populations, many of whom hold influential positions in government, universities and the local media. Nonetheless, many of these states have very different attitudes toward the Arab-Israel conflict. In some, it will be argued, even were an agreeable solution to the conflict to be found, it would still be doubtful whether they would change their attitudes substantially toward granting the US military facilities.

In the Gulf region itself, the GCC states may be more or less in agreement on the need for certain minimal Arab conditions to be met in an Arab-Israel settlement. But they differ markedly over whether to allow their attitudes toward Israel to affect their relations with third parties who advance other policies. The most outstanding example in the Gulf, in this respect, is Oman — the only Gulf state to have granted the US access to its military facilities. Oman never cut off its diplomatic relations with Egypt throughout the Camp David peace process leading up to the March 1979 peace treaty. Its reserve in attacking third parties for their different views of the Arab-Israel conflict has also been evident in the Omani press, which has not only been supportive of Egypt and the US, but most recently of Morocco as well.

Oman's relatively tolerant attitude toward states maintaining or initiating contacts with Israel is a function of several factors. First, unlike the other Gulf states, the Omani leadership has no large foreign Palestinian community to take into account. Whether due to the fact that the Palestinian presence is miniscule or due to other considerations of high policy, Oman is one of the few Arab states with no PLO office. A second factor affecting Omani policy toward third parties is that Oman has adopted a highly pragmatic approach to the peace process that does not seem burdened with ideology or rhetoric. In a somewhat bold interview given to the Kuwaiti daily *al-Anba'* in September 1985, Omani Minister of State for Foreign Affairs Yusuf al-'Alawi declared:

> ...in the end there will be direct negotiations between Palestinians and Israelis. This issue has always been discussed from an Arab point of view and with Arab perception, and we have never tried to understand the Israeli point of view and perceptions. In the end the Palestinian people have rights and Israel's people have rights.[18]

Had these words been uttered by Sultan Qabus, they might have more significance. Nonetheless, in most Arab states — excluding Egypt — a foreign minister who made such a pronouncement in the Arab press would probably be relieved of his position. Yusuf al-'Alawi continued to be Oman's foreign minister.

Given this background of Omani policy and attitudes, it would be difficult to claim that US links with Israel complicate US strategic cooperation with the only Gulf state to have granted the US access to its facilities. As discussed in the previous chapter, Oman may in the future have its own reasons for lowering the profile of its strategic relations with the United States, whether due to its changing relationship with PDRY and the USSR or because it prefers to act within the policy-framework of the GCC.

Moreover, Oman has a non-communist alternative to the US, especially in low intensity warfare scenarios: Great Britain. With British officers seconded to Oman in key military positions and British advisers serving the civilian government, there may be an internal lobby in Muscat influencing Oman's choices as well. While there have been no public disclosures of any USCENTCOM maneuvers in Oman since the early 1980s, British airborne and seaborne troops conducted a large exercise in Oman called "Swift Sword" in November 1986. This, despite active British support for the US raid on Libya in April 1986, the recall of Britain's ambassador to Damascus, and Prime Minister Thatcher's visit to Israel — all terrible offenses to extreme Arab nationalist sentiment.[19]

It could be argued that the United States is interested in broadening its access to facilities in the Gulf beyond Oman, and that for such an expansion to become feasible Israeli policies must change in order to relieve the US of the stigma of being perceived as Israel's prime backer. Further, one might contend that while the US-Israeli connection has not blocked the US-Omani relationship, the Omani exception in the Gulf merely proves the rule — that there *is* a connection between the Arab-Israel conflict and access to facilities: only Oman, with its more liberal attitude toward Israel, was ready to give the US limited strategic rights. But for the other Gulf states, including Saudi Arabia, it is no longer clear that a settlement of the conflict involving major Israeli concessions is a precondition for the advancement of US security interests. Despite their continued declaratory anti-Israel policies, in 1987 they went a long way toward separating their opinions on the Arab-Israel conflict from issues of Gulf security. As a result of the November 1987 Amman summit, they joined the ranks of Oman by reestablishing diplomatic relations with Egypt. Nor did Egyptian policy toward Israel change; rather, the intensification of the Iranian threat to the GCC led to a reduction in the impact of the Arab-Israel conflict on GCC states' ties with important third parties. Similarly, improvements in US military access to the Gulf states were not made conditional on any modification of US policy toward the Arab-Israel conflict or the Palestinian issue.

Once the Iranian threat diminishes, however, will not the GCC states again assert the linkage between the Arab-Israel conflict and US military access to the Gulf? But under such conditions it is by no means apparent that a solution to the conflict would modify

Saudi or other GCC state policies regarding a US military presence. Saudi Arabia as well as some of the other Gulf states have in the past carefully adapted their position on the Arab-Israel conflict to the demands of the Arab consensus, so as to avoid deep polarization of the Arab world that would force them to choose sides. Even if an Arab-Israel settlement could be reached, Saudi Arabia would probably continue to follow consensus-building policies. If any of the principal Arab powers, such as Syria, were to oppose the outcome of direct Arab-Israel negotiations, it would be doubtful that Saudi Arabia could simply ignore such a minority Arab position. Because a settlement will undoubtedly produce some dissatisfied parties, the Saudis and their smaller Gulf allies may not so easily agree to its terms; Saudi consensus-building policies might very well prohibit open acceptance of Israel. Thus, paradoxically, should Arab concessions in the settlement be seen as resulting from positions taken by the US, an Arab-Israel settlement could actually even further complicate US access to regional facilities.

Moreover, after the passing of the Iranian threat to the Gulf states, several other factors might make themselves felt again, and these could well inhibit US-Gulf state cooperation — without any connection to the Arab-Israel conflict. The GCC may well revert to asserting its declaratory policies of non-alignment. For a country like Kuwait, non-alignment is not a matter of rhetoric, but a traditional national security policy that seeks to maintain good relations with the USSR as well — especially in light of the latter's leverage over its past (and possibly future) threatening neighbor: Iraq. A number of GCC states believed in the past that by openly granting military facilities in the Gulf to one superpower they could generate hostile countermeasures by the other superpower, leading to a destabilizing eruption of superpower competition throughout the region.

Aside from these global considerations, the GCC may well still be motivated by strong regional factors limiting its military cooperation with the US. For example, the undercurrent of Islamic hostility to a western military presence on Arab/Islamic soil has been a powerful cause for limiting the magnitude of US forces in the region. This element has been especially important for Saudi Arabia as the protector of Islam's two most holy cities — Mecca and Medina. A large US military presence in Saudi Arabia lends credibility to the charge that non-Muslims are desecrating the

Hijaz — the Islamic Holy Land. Saudi Arabia is especially sensitive to any criticism about its capacity to be the protector of the Hijaz.

At least three conclusions may be drawn from the previous analysis. *First*, it is difficult to accept Cordesman's special focus on US-Israel relations as the *principal* limiting factor in the emergence of a full strategic partnership between the Gulf states and the US. Cordesman does not specify what precisely that partnership consists of. Certainly, if it involves the development of a regional environment more hospitable to the peacetime US military interests of CENTCOM, then there are many other factors, at least as important, that inhibit the full development of a US military partnership with the Gulf. Moreover, Cordesman's generalizations about Gulf state responses to US-Israel relations do not take into account the special case of Oman — which after all is the only Gulf state that has an explicit agreement granting the United States use of its facilities under agreed special conditions. Certainly in the Omani case, it is a little far-fetched to assert that the US relationship with Israel "threaten(s) any Gulf state that allies itself to the US." Oman has not become any more vulnerable by virtue of its 1980 arrangements with the US.

Secondly, among the several factors affecting US-Gulf state relations, the Arab-Israel complex appears to be a *declining* factor. This development is due to the Egyptian-Israeli peace treaty and the growing strategic dependence of Iraq and the GCC states on Egypt because of the Iran-Iraq War. The November 1987 Amman summit and the restoration of diplomatic relations between Egypt and the GCC states attest to this change. Even when disturbances erupted in the West Bank and Gaza Strip in December 1987, they appeared to impinge mostly on relations between Israelis and Palestinians, rather than on the entire Middle East region. They certainly did not disturb the US military presence in the Persian Gulf.

A *third* set of conclusions that may be drawn from the previous analysis relates to whether an Arab-Israel peace settlement would create the prerequisite conditions for the emergence of a US-Arabian Peninsula security bloc, that would be far more hospitable to US military requirements. Cordesman, while recognizing that a peace settlement would reduce American policy dilemmas, hardly suggests that an Arab-Israel settlement would be a panacea leading to the realization of US strategic goals in the Gulf area. But the assertion that an Arab-Israel peace must *precede* the emergence of a pro-US security system has been made so often in the history of American Middle East policy, that it has to be examined here as well. Unfortunately, a full Arab-Israel peace may not be realized for a long time. Strategic planners who hope that a more active future administration, by nudging the peace process further, may improve US military access to the Gulf region, may have a long wait ahead. If anything, the principal factor that might open up the GCC states to an enhanced US regional presence on their soil will be a clear regional threat against their sovereignty. This became evident in 1987 as the Iranian threat, more than any other recent regional development, seemed to be altering the receptivity of the Gulf states to US forces and protection.

Toward a Model of Strategic Consensus

How might Israel be associated with an American strategic structure in the Middle East that comprised those Arab states politically and militarily oriented toward the West? No one could expect that Israel and pro-western Arab states would in the near future freely associate themselves in a pro-western Middle East collective security alliance. In any case, the United States is now at the end of the 1980s and not in the middle of the 1950s; no one in Washington is building Dulles-style pacts around the Soviet periphery any more. Taken together, a more sophisticated Soviet diplomatic style in the Arab world, including an increasing interest in the Gulf in particular, and ongoing Arab nationalist sensitivities to western alliances and any foreign military presence, render NATO-style alliance-modeling in the Middle East largely a theoretical exercise with no practical application.

It is unfortunate that former Secretary of State Haig's concept of "strategic consensus" got such bad reviews in 1981 when it was first advanced. All that was attempted by the use of this term was to recognize that certain common international security problems had arisen in the Middle East that threatened Arabs and Israelis alike, and that greater mutual understanding might be achieved if many of these common challenges were recognized by both parties. Two perceptions arose in connection with the concept that led to its rejection in certain Arab quarters. First, that strategic consensus was some kind of seedling for the kind of explicit multilateral alliance structure embracing Israel and the Arab states that is described above. Secondly, that the mutual threat that ultimately formed the consensus emanated from the USSR. Viewed strictly in these terms the strategic consensus concept never had much of a chance.

The previous analysis has demonstrated that security threats common to Israel and many Arab states have historically arisen and have led, at different times, to mutual strategic interests and even tacit forms of strategic cooperation. Without the public fanfare of a Middle East tour by a US secretary of state, these mutual interests ought to be recognized by the United States and communicated to both sides. Moreover, any strategic dialogue between the US on the one hand, and Israel and the Arab states on the other, ought to seek to explain how US actions are intended to support what may at times be the mutual interests of Arabs and Israelis alike. Cordesman recognizes such a need when he notes that one reason why Israel has reacted strongly in the past to proposed American weapons-sales packages to Saudi Arabia is related to the way Israel was informed of the American decision:

> There is a need for more forthright US efforts to communicate to Israel the rationale for given US arms sales to the Gulf states. It is not fair to blame Israel, or the various US political groups that support Israel, for all of Israel's overreaction to the AWACS package or its resistance to any long-term expansion of US ties to the conservative Gulf states. The US has made far too little effort to develop a process of tacit communication among its major allies in the Near East or to encourage their understanding of the degree to which a modus vivendi among them can serve a common interest and create a true "strategic consensus."[20]

Cordesman is essentially prescribing a formula for interim US policy toward both sides. Once peace is realized, communications will no longer have to be tacit.

For purposes of this study, the practical question that arises is whether the United States can facilitate a modus vivendi between Israel and the conservative states of the Gulf — and above all, Saudi Arabia — by having them separated by different US unified commands. Each side needs to understand the strategic threats and priorities of the other. Who better could explain to Israel the importance of a particular American advanced weapons system for a western-oriented Arab state — as well as American influence on its deployment or transferability — than the unified command which is responsible for security assistance programs in its AOR?

Having a mechanism that places Israel and Arab states friendly to the United States in the same area of responsibility of a US unified command thus serves to facilitate a subtle form of strategic consensus. It does not impose on Arab states joint membership with Israel in a multilateral alliance. CENTCOM, after all, is not CENTO or the Middle East Command; it is only a subdivision of the US military establishment. It should not bother most conservative Arab states whether they are located in the same subdivision with Israel or not; after all, Israel is not separated from those very same states by being placed under a separate bureau of the Department of State. Those who, in any case, might object to seeing CENTCOM develop a relationship with Israel as well, might shortly afterwards realize the benefits accruing from increased tacit communication among the region's states.

It might also be worthwhile for American planners to consider the possible positive interaction between the formation of such a strategic consensus and the Arab-Israel peace process. One of the Israeli architects of Israel's peace strategy, Major General (res.) Abraham Tamir, has written that the long-term goal of Israel's diplomacy should be a final stable peace based on its integration into a regional economic-security system; under such conditions he proposes that it may very well be possible to separate Israel's political, economic, and security borders.[21]

Without relating to the specifics of Tamir's proposals, his plan recognizes the inter-relationship between regional security systems and stable peace structures. Certainly, the emergence of the NATO alliance has constrained conflict in Europe, whether between past rivals like France and Germany, or current ones like Greece and Turkey. The involvement of Israel in a strategic consensus in the Middle East, as already noted, does not entail the placement of Israel and the Arab states in an explicit alliance system. It does, however, establish low-profile channels of communication that can enhance understanding and contribute to conflict restraint. Should changes arise in the Middle Eastern threat environment that cause CENTCOM eventually to require an explicit security structure similar to that found in Western Europe, then this strategic consensus could serve as the basis for such a future regional alliance grouping.

In sum, Israel's exclusion from CENTCOM's AOR presents

certain difficulties for US-Israel cooperation in contingencies to Israel's east. Mechanisms exist in the unified command system for mitigating cross-command coordination. American planners would be well advised to examine whether those mechanisms are sufficiently developed in the Israel-CENTCOM case. In another sector of CENTCOM's AOR, the Straits of Hormuz, cross-command coordination was apparently insufficiently developed to allow the division of US Gulf forces between CENTCOM and PACOM; thus PACOM's out-of-area units were placed under CENTCOM control. Whether placing Israel in CENTCOM for certain contingencies would similarly improve American *military* effectiveness in the Middle East is a subject that planners ought to consider. Here it is argued that the *political* limitations that are often cited in placing Israel in the same area of responsibility as the conservative Arab states are frequently overstated.

In the course of the 1980s the Arab world has come to accept US-Israeli strategic cooperation: from Sixth Fleet port visits to joint work on SDI. By the late '80s, Arab preoccupation with the Iranian threat had lessened Gulf state involvement in the Palestinian problem; movement on a Palestinian solution was no longer presented as a prior condition to US-GCC cooperation. If anything, the link between the Arab-Israel conflict and Gulf security has hurt the GCC states by serving to block US arms sales to countries failing to support the peace process.

6. Conclusions: Changing Patterns of US Military Interaction

From the perspective of US defense planning, the establishment and development of CENTCOM in the course of the 1980s represent a fundamental change in the postwar pattern of US military interaction with the Middle East. First, beginning with a core interest in the defense of the oil-producing areas of the Persian Gulf, the advent of CENTCOM has led to the definition of a new military-geographic zone, known as Southwest Asia, and the planning of that area's security in a unified manner. Past US military plans for the defense of the region were often piecemeal. Though it preferred to preserve allied — initially British-strategic — responsibility for the Middle East, the United States in an almost ad hoc manner was forced to plug the holes in the area's defense as the British executed a series of military withdrawals in the early postwar period.

Secondly, in the immediate postwar years American planners were concerned with the possibility of a direct Soviet overland threat to the Middle East. After the mid-1950s the US began to focus its attention on the threat emanating from Soviet-supported states in the area. Since direct Soviet aggression was assumed to lead to general war between the superpowers, US nuclear predominance became an important factor in checking the threat of direct Soviet expansionism. But by the 1980s, the problem of deterring direct Soviet military expansion in the Middle East had returned as the major preoccupation of US planners. Thus, whereas STRICOM was conceived briefly in the early 1960s for lower scale "brushfire" contingencies against Soviet proxies in the Third World, CENTCOM was structured in the 1980s for handling direct threats from the USSR. The Soviet invasion of Afghanistan proved what American strategic planners had already theorized about: that the advent of nuclear parity had altered the credibility of any American nuclear threat against Soviet aggression in non-NATO (and perhaps non-Northeast Asia) scenarios. A conventional US deterrent was necessary to at least bolster the ultimate nuclear threat as in Europe, and eventually to replace it. Moreover, since US-Soviet confrontations in the Middle East, under these new strategic conditions, could be conceivable without escalation to global general war, regional balances of power between the superpowers acquired new relevance.

Third, the need for a conventional deterrent for direct Soviet provocations affected the kind of force-mix thought appropriate for projecting American power in the region. Historically, the peacetime presence of the US in the Middle East and its adjacent waters developed from an initial projection of US naval power to the deployment of US air power as well. The predominant role of the US Navy and the US Air Force in Middle Eastern defense was reflected in wartime operational plans in the 1950s as well. US global war plans for most of the 1950s did not envision any role for American ground forces in the Middle East. Rather, they relied on local, Middle Eastern ground forces for major anti-Soviet and lesser anti-proxy contingencies. In the aftermath of the Eisenhower Doctrine the US Army came to have a greater say in Middle Eastern planning. The creation of STRICOM seemed to signify a possible new role for the US Army in the Middle East, but the manpower requirements of the Vietnam War assured that this new mission could not be so easily assumed.

The revolution in US military interaction with the Middle East caused by the creation of CENTCOM reflects not only the fact that all the armed services are now engaged in planning and training for the defense of the region, but, more specifically, that the Army's ground forces are fully involved. While the peacetime deployments of US forces in the CENTCOM AOR are still chiefly those of the US Navy and the US Air Force, growing American strategic mobility capabilities and repeated regional exercises are giving the US Army a certain degree of presence in the region well above the level that might have been felt in previous decades. Thus, while an American "tripwire" is not in place in Iran as it is in West Germany, Soviet planners must consider that with strategic warning such a force could be deployed, and that its destruction by an invading Soviet army would have the gravest implications for US decisionmakers. By the end of the 1980s and the beginning of the 1990s, substantially larger ground forces than those envisioned in any tripwire force might become rapidly deployable, as well. Correspondingly, like in NATO-Europe, as the US Army's capability to balance Soviet conventional superiority on the ground grows, the nuclear threshold in any Soviet-American confrontation in the CENTCOM region could be considerably raised.

The fourth change associated with the creation of CENTCOM is connected with the strategic importance of the Middle East itself to the United States. Despite diplomatic and congressional fanfare over the decades on the Arab-Israel issue, the Middle East has historically been a strategic vacuum for the United States, for reasons explained in Chapter 2. A succession of events in the 1970s, beginning with the energy crisis and ending with the fall of the Shah of Iran and the Soviet invasion of Afghanistan, demanded a revision of American strategic thinking about the area. The defense of the Persian Gulf has since become one of the pillars of US defense policy, along with the defense of NATO-Europe and Northeast Asia. A limiting factor in the assumption of these responsibilities is certainly the number of Army divisions, Air Force wings, Navy carrier task forces, and Marine units already committed to EUCOM and PACOM missions. But if past American patterns are any indication, should a crisis develop in the Gulf region alone, the US may dip into forces assigned elsewhere in order to execute CENTCOM's mission. Thus although the growth of the overall size of the US Armed Forces in the 1980s does not reflect the full implications of the addition of the Southwest Asia mission, the perennial problem of inadequate resources for US commitments should not necessarily preclude increasing US involvement in Southwest Asia.

From the US perspective alone, these strategic changes point to conversion of large parts of the Middle East into a strategic zone with increasing similarities to NATO-Europe. Certainly the American goal of rapidly deploying ground forces in the region requires a local infrastructure to support the massive logistical requirements of the US Army and, to a lesser extent, the US Air Force. But unlike the situation in NATO-Europe or Northeast Asia, no US treaty structure with the states of the region supports the American military mission. Certainly under peacetime conditions there exist no political understandings that might permit the ongoing deployment in the Middle East of force levels even remotely comparable with US forces stationed in Western Europe.

In fact, if there is a constant point in the pattern of US military interaction with the Middle East from the 1950s to the 1980s, it is the tendency of America's local partners in the area to be more concerned with intra-regional conflict than with the Soviet threat. This has led to a situation where many of CENTCOM's regionally deployed assets have come to deter regional conflicts — or their expansion — as well as provide a minimal rudimentary infrastructure for anti-Soviet scenarios. Despite this utility, the states in the core area of CENTCOM's AOR — those belonging to the Gulf Cooperation Council — find it difficult openly to make common cause with the United States, as evidenced by their behavior at different phases of the Tanker War in the Iran-Iraq conflict. This reluctance was modified in 1987 due to the US reflagging and convoy mission of Kuwaiti tankers. But even in this case GCC readiness to grant the US military access was only granted grudgingly, on a piecemeal basis. Moreover, these concessions to US military forces were shrouded in secrecy. Open deployment of a US *land-based* deterrent force did not result from the enhanced Iranian threat. The development of a regional security system modeled on the NATO example to support CENTCOM's mission — even when a mutually agreed threat arises — remained as remote a possibility in the late 1980s as it was in the 1950s.

It has been common wisdom in Washington to assume that as soon as the Arab-Israel conflict is solved, a pro-western regional security system may become more of a possibility, since the US will no longer be tainted by supporting "Zionist expansionism." If anything, the previous analysis has shown that many reasons — aside from the undeniable opposition of many states in the Arabian Peninsula to Israel and its policies — block the formation of a Middle Eastern NATO. That should not become a reason for halting the pursuit of peace in the area. It should, however, direct American security planners away from a tendency to wait for the peace process to come to fruition. The real question for US security plans in the Middle East in the next decade is what the US should and can do until peace comes. Yet even after peace, security planning for the area will have to take into account traditional sensitivities among the weaker states in the CENTCOM area to any foreign military presence, and their fears lest their region be converted into a stage for superpower rivalry.

CENTCOM strategies in the 1990s will have to utilize technological and tactical innovations in order to be effective in such a politically sensitive zone. Moreover, any regional security system will have to rest more on tacit understandings than on explicit international treaties. One such understanding that the GCC states might be ready for is the delinkage of the Arab-Israel conflict from the question of Gulf security. The link between the two has served as a major factor preventing GCC states from acquiring sophisticated military equipment from the United States just when they have had to face the immediate threat of a spillover from the Iran-Iraq War. As much as GCC support for the peace process might be appreciated, it is unrealistic to expect these relatively weak Arab consensus-builders to stick their necks out in that process.

On the other hand, any tacit agreement by Israel to look aside when major weapons systems are sold to states that might choose to enter a future war coalition, requires a certain concession from the other side. If Gulf security and the Arab-Israel conflict are to be decoupled, they must be decoupled in all aspects. Thus, were the US to integrate Israel more fully into defense strategies in the CENTCOM area, and thereby more fully realize their mutual strategic interests, the GCC states or their pragmatic Egyptian and Jordanian partners should not make that change conditional on a full resolution of the Arab-Israel conflict. Moreover, the ongoing military threat projected by the Islamic Republic of Iran has slowly brought about a convergence of Sunni Arab and Israeli strategic interests, as evidenced by Israel's readiness during 1987 to reconsider its historic strategic ties with Tehran. If a link between Gulf security and the Arab-Israel conflict exists, then it in fact ought to be encouraged — as in fact it bespeaks the emergence of the "strategic convergence" just described. An environment in which Israel and its Sunni Arab neighbors develop a strategic dialogue based on a mutual Iranian threat should facilitate new political understandings that were previously beyond their capacity.

The problems of Soviet conventional superiority in areas adjacent to the Middle East in an era of nuclear parity will continue into the 1990s. As the Middle East is the only zone along the periphery of the borders of the Soviet Bloc — aside from Communist China — that is not covered by the American treaty umbrella — it will continue to be a zone of temptation to the USSR and an area of probable US-Soviet rivalry. Even if, as is likely, Soviet remote power projection capabilities into Southern Africa or Central America remain limited until the end of the century, it should not be beyond Soviet military capabilities to project conventional forces a thousand miles south of the Soviet border. Whether or not Gorbachev is initiating a new era in East-West relations, these strategic realities point to a continued need for CENTCOM's mission.

In the past the Soviet Union allied itself with forces in the Middle

East that were anxious to alter the region's political status quo. Alternatively, more recently it has offered conservative Arab states the leverage it appears to have over the Middle Estern states that threaten them. Whether the USSR follows the older or the newer pattern in the future, regional instability in the Middle East is likely to continue. Local states will continue to need American support in order to promote regional stability. The United States can provide that support directly by deploying limited force multipliers, like AWACS, to the area at times of regional crises.

The US can also promote mutual understandings between parties facing similar threats. In the past Israel has faced identical threats to those of many Arab regimes friendly with the United States. The existence of tacit understandings regarding these mutual threats should be encouraged — and not avoided by separating Israel from many of its neighbors in distinct areas of responsibility. American intervention in more conventional regional conflicts might be avoided by encouraging local balances of power against regionally ambitious states. In the 1990s both Israel and its pro-western Arab rivals should try to pursue a policy of "live and let live." They should quietly promote American strength in the Middle East and avoid trying to place conditions on American friendship with the other side.

Notes

Chapter 2

1.   Raymond Aron, "From Yankee Imperialism to Russian Hegemony? Turning Points in World Politics," Encounter 2, no. 2 (August 1979).

2.   Alexander George and Richard Smoke, Deterrence in American Foreign Policy Theory and Practice (New York: Columbia University Press, 1974), p. 80.

3.   J.C. Hurewitz, The Middle East and North Africa in World Politics: A Documentary Record, Volume 2, British-French Supremacy, 1914-1945 (New Haven and London: Yale University Press, 1979). See author's analytic introduction to Document 138, p. 589.   Maurice Matloff and Edwin M. Snell, Strategic Planning for Coalition Warfare, 1941-1942 (Office of the Chief of Military History, Department of the Army, Washington, 1953), chapters 7 and 11.

4.   Memorandum prepared in the Department of State, "The British and American Positions." US Department of State: Historical Office. Foreign Relations of the United States, 1947, Volume III (Washington: US Government Printing Office), p. 514.

5.   When the Office of Near Eastern and African Affairs was created in the 'Department of State in 1944, it included a Division of Near Eastern Affairs with responsibility for Greece and Turkey. Other divisions included the Division of Middle Eastern and Indian Affairs and the Division of African Affairs. See Bruce R. Kuniholm, The Origins of the Cold War in the Near East: Great Power Conflict and Diplomacy in Iran, Turkey, and Greece (Princeton: Princeton University Press, 1980). Appendix A, p. 433.

6.   Ibid., Appendix B, pp. 434-439.

7.   US National Archives (Washington DC), RG 218. Records of the United States Joint Chiefs of Staff. The Joint Chiefs of Staff and National Policy, 1947-49, Volume 2 (1976), pp. 41-56.

8.   Lieutenant Alan Majorano, US Navy, "A Fresh Look at the Sixth Fleet," US Naval Institute Proceedings, February 1984, p. 52.

9.   Report by the Joint Strategic Plans Committee to the Joint Chiefs of Staff.   "Military Viewpoint Regarding the Eastern Mediterranean and the Middle East Area," JCS 1997/1 (19 July 1948) in Paul Kesaris, ed., Records of the Joint Chiefs of Staff, Part 2, 1946-1953, The Middle East.

10. Memorandum by the Assistant Secretary of State for Near Eastern, South Asian and African Affairs to the Secretary of State. Annex 1: "Re-evaluation of US Plans for the Middle East," Foreign Relations of the United States, 1951, Volume V (Washington: US Government Printing Office, 1982), p. 6.

11. Statement of Policy Proposal by the National Security Council, March 14, 1951. Foreign Relations of the United States, 1951, Volume V, p. 95.

12. US National Archives (Washington DC), RG 218. Records of the

Joint Chiefs of Staff. <u>The Joint Chiefs of Staff and National Policy 1950-1952</u>, Volume IV, pp. 367-375.

13. John C. Campbell, <u>Defense of the Middle East: Problems of American Policy</u> (New York: Praeger Publishers, 1960), p. 39.

14. Paul Y. Hammond, "NSC-68: Prologue to Rearmament," in Warner Schilling, Paul Y. Hammond, and Glenn H. Snyder, <u>Strategy, Politics, and Defense Budgets</u> (New York: Columbia University Press, 1962), pp. 271-330.

15. "Military Requirements for the Defense of the Middle East" (A Briefing by the Chairman, Joint Chiefs of Staff for the Deputy Secretary of Defense) JCS 1887/61, November 26, 1952, in Paul Kenaris (ed.) <u>Records of the Joint Chiefs of Staff</u>, Part 2, 1946-53, The Middle East.

16. "Department of State Minutes of State--Joint Chiefs of Staff Meeting," June 18, 1982, in <u>Foreign Relations of the United States</u>, 1952-1954, "The Near and Middle East," Part 1 (Washington: US Government Printing Office, 1986), p. 246.

17. "Re-evaluation of US Plans for the Middle East."

18. "State Department Draft Minutes of Discussions at the State --Joint Chiefs of Staff Meeting," January 30, 1951, in <u>Foreign Relations of the United States</u>, 1951, Volume V, The Near East and Africa (Washington: US Government Printing Office, 1982), p. 33.

19. "Re-evaluation of US Plans for the Middle East" and "Statement of Policy Proposed by the National Security Council," NSC 47/5, March 14, 1951, in <u>Foreign Relations of the United States</u>, 1951, Volume V, p. 95.

20. <u>Ibid</u>.

21. <u>The Joint Chiefs of Staff and National Policy, 1950-1952</u>, Volume IV, pp. 331-378.

22. "Department of State Minutes of State--Joint Chiefs of Staff Meeting," June 18, 1952, <u>Foreign Relations of the United States</u>, 1952-1954, p. 246.

23. Glenn H. Snyder, "The New Look of 1953," in Warner Schilling, Paul Hammond, and Glenn Snyder.

24. Report by the Joint Strategic Plans Committee in Collaboration with the Joint Logistics Plans Committee and the Joint Intelligence Committee, "Defense of the Middle East," JCS 1887/70, October 13, 1953, in Paul Kesaris (ed.).

25. Campbell, <u>Defense of the Middle East</u>, p. 187.

26. Note by the Executive Secretary to the National Security Council, "Basic National Security Policy," NSC 162/1, October 30, 1953, in <u>The Pentagon Papers: The Defense Department History of United States Decisionmaking on Vietnam</u>. Senator Gravel Edition, Volume I (Boston: Beacon Press, 1971), p. 415.

27. US National Archives (Washington DC), RG 218, Records of the United States Joint Chiefs of Staff. <u>The Joint Chiefs of Staff and National Policy</u>, chapter 8, "The Eisenhower Doctrine and Middle East Plans," pp. 416-417.

28. Campbell, <u>Defense of the Middle East</u>, p. 123.

29. <u>Ibid</u>., p. 171 (see footnote 5).

30. US National Archives (Washington DC), RG 218. Records of the United States Joint Chiefs of Staff. <u>The Joint Chiefs of Staff and National Policy</u>, chapter 9, "The Lebanon Crisis and After," p. 475.

31. <u>Ibid</u>.

32. The Joint Chiefs of Staff and National Policy, chapter 9, p. 452.

33. Ibid., pp. 428, 483.

34. General Paul D. Adams, US Army. "Strike Command," Military Review, Volume XLII, no. 5 (May 1962). Robert P. Haffa, Jr., The Half War: Planning US Rapid Deployment Forces to Meet a Limited Contingency, 1960-1983 (Boulder, Colorado: Westview Press, 1984), pp. 93-106. See also General Bruce Palmer, Jr., The 25-Year War: America's Military Role in Vietnam (Lexington, Kentucky: The University Press of Kentucky, 1984), p. 137.

35. Henry Kissinger, White House Years (Boston: Little, Brown, 1979), p. 605.

36. US Congress, House of Representatives, Committee on Foreign Affairs, Subcommittee on the Near East and South Asia. Hearings, New Perspectives on the Persian Gulf, 93rd Congress, 1st Session, 1973 (Washington: Government Printing Offce), p. 39.

37. Melvin R. Laird, The Nixon Doctrine (Washington DC: The American Enterprise Institute, 1972), pp. 9-10.

38. Kissinger, White House Years, pp. 605-606.

39. Haffa, The Half War, pp. 105-107.

Chapter 3

1. Zbigniew Brzezinski, Power and Principle: Memoirs of the National Security Adviser 1977-1981 (New York: Farrar, Straus, Giroux, 1983), pp. 455.

2. John Joseph Stocker, "Rapid Deployment Forces. Issue Brief No. 1B80027," in US Congress, Senate, Committee on Foreign Relations, Subcommittee on Near Eastern and South Asian Affairs, Hearings, US Security Interests and Policies in Southwest Asia, 96th Congress, 2nd Session, 1980 (Washington DC: US Government Printing Office), p. 327.

3. Ibid.

4. David E. Long, The United States and Saudi Arabia: Ambivalent Allies (Boulder, Colorado: Westview Press, 1985), p. 62.

5. William Quandt, "The Middle East Crises," in Foreign Affairs, America and the World 1979, Volume 58, no. 3, p. 543.

6. US Department of Defense (FY 1980).

7. International Herald Tribune, December 16, 1986.

8. Baltimore Sun, March 18, 1979; New York Times, June 28, 1979.

9. Christian Science Monitor, June 22, 1979.

10. Harold Brown, Thinking About National Security: Defense and Foreign Policy in a Dangerous World (Boulder, Colorado: Westview Press, 1983), p. 746.

11. Haffa, The Half War, p. 119.

12. Ibid., p. 126.

13. A Discussion of the Rapid Deployment Force with Lieutenant General P.X. Kelly. AEI Special Analyses (Washington DC: American Enterprise Institute).

14. Washington Post, June 6, 1986.

15. International Herald Tribune, April 4 and August 27., 1980;

Anthony Cordesman, The Gulf and the Search for Strategic Stability: Saudi Arabia, The Military Balance in the Gulf, and Trends in the Arab-Israeli Military Balance (Boulder, Colorado: Westview Press, 1984), p. 835.
16. New York Times, September 14, 1980.
17. International Herald Tribune, April 4, 1980.
18. Maxwell Johnson, The Military as an Instrument of US Policy in Southwest Asia: The Rapid Deployment Joint Task Force, 1979-1982 (Boulder, Colorado: Westview Press, 1983), p. 25.
19. Nadav Safran, Saudi Arabia: The Ceaseless Quest for Security (Cambridge, Mass: Belknap Press/Harvard University Press, 1985), pp. 208-209, 447.
20. Johnson, The Military as an Instrument, pp. 68-80.
21. International Herald Tribune, November 14, 1980.
22. "Statement of General George B. Crist, US Marine Corps Commander-in-Chief US Central Command Before the Senate Armed Services Committee on the Status of the United States Central Command." March 11, 1986, pp. 26-39.
23. Ibid., p. 25.
24. Washington Post, January 13, 1987.
25. US Department of Defense, Soviet Military Power, 1987 (Washington DC: US Department of Defense), p. 70.
26. Vice Admiral W.J. Crowe, US Navy. "The Persian Gulf: Central or Peripheral to United States Strategy?" US Naval Institute Proceedings, May 1978, p. 204.
27. Fred Ikle and Albert Wohlstetter (cochairmen), Discriminate Deterrence, Report of the Commission on Integrated Long-Term Strategy (Washington: US Government Printing Office, January 1988), pp. 43, 23.
28. "Statement of General George Crist," p. 75.
29. Jeffrey Record, The Rapid Deployment Force and US Military Intervention in the Persian Gulf (Washington DC: Institute for Foreign Policy Analysis, 1983), p. 54. DOD Annual Reports FY 1984, FY 1987.
30. Raphael Iungerich, "US Rapid Deployment Forces--US CENTCOM--What is it? Can It Do the Job?" in Armed Forces Journal, October 1984.
31. "National Security Strategy of the United States" (Part Three: Reagan Administration Report to Congress), February 2, 1987. Backgrounder, United States Information Service, p. 12.
32. DOD Annual Report, FY 1984.
33. Jeffrey Record, "Jousting with Unreality: Reagan's Military Strategy," International Security 8, no. 3 (Winter 1983/84), p. 16.
34. John M. Collins, Clyde R. Mark, Elizabeth Ann Severns, "Petroleum Imports from the Persian Gulf: Use of US Armed Force to Ensure Supplies." Issue Brief No. IB79046, US Congress, Senate Committee on Foreign Relations, Subcommittee on Near Eastern and South Asian Affairs. US Security Interests and Policies in Southwest Asia. 96th Congress, Second Session. February-March 1980, pp. 336-366.
35. Christian Science Monitor, January 16, 1986.
36. Michael J. Crutchley, "The Light Infantry: A Status Report," Military Technology, no. 10/86 (October 1986), pp. 56-65.
37. Colin S. Gray and Jeffrey G. Barlow, "Inexcusable Restraint:

The Decline of American Military Power in the 1970s,"
International Security 10, no. 2 (Fall 1985), p. 63.

38. Department of Defense, *Report of the Secretary of Defense Caspar W. Weinberger to the Congress on the FY 1987, FY 1988 Authorization Request and FY 1987-1991 Defense Programs* (Washington DC: US Government Printing Office, 1986), p. 156.
39. Ibid., p. 155.
40. Ibid., p. 156.
41. Crutchley, "The Light Infantry," p. 61.
42. Kenneth Waltz, "A Strategy for the Rapid Deployment Force," *International Security* 5, no. 4 (Spring 1981), p. 59.
43. Brzezinski, *Power and Principle*, p. 445.
44. Waltz, "A Strategy for the Rapid Deployment Force," p. 66.
45. Joshua M. Epstein, "Horizontal Escalation: Sour Notes of a Recurrent Theme," *International Security* 8, no. 3 (Winter 1983-84), pp. 22-23.
46. Jeffrey Record, *US Strategic Airlift: Requirements and Capabilities* (Cambridge, Mass. and Washington DC: Institute for Foreign Policy Program, 1986).
47. Scott C. Turner, "Sealift for the Overseas Connection," *Armed Forces Journal*, August 1986; Jack Phelps, "Sealift," *International Combat Arms*, May 1987.
48. Thomas L. McNaugher, *Arms and Oil: US Military Strategy and the Persian Gulf* (Washington DC: The Brookings Institution, 1985), pp. 64-65.
49. Joshua Epstein, "Soviet Vulnerabilities in Iran and the RDF Deterrent," *International Security* 6, no. 2 (1981), pp. 126-158.
50. Brzezinski, *Power and Principle*, p. 454.
51. *Rapid Deployment Forces: Policy and Budgetary Implications* (Washington DC: Congressional Budget Office, 1983), p. 8.
52. Record, "Jousting with Unreality," p. 6.
53. *US News and World Report*, December 24, 1984.
54. Caspar W. Weinberger, *A Report to the Congress on Security Arrangements in the Persian Gulf*, June 15, 1987.

Chapter 4

1. Stephen Kaplan and Barry Blechman, *Force Without War* (Washington: The Brookings Institution, 1978), p. 101.
2. Statement of General George Crist, p. 64.
3. Ibid.
4. Ibid., p. 67.
5. Ibid.
6. Ibid., p. 68.
7. Colin Legum and Haim Shaked (ed.), *Middle East Contemporary Survey* (hereafter, *MECS*), 1978-79, p. 436.
8. Ibid.
9. *MECS*, 1980-81, p. 463.
10. Ibid., pp. 740-741.
11. Ibid., p. 463; see also *US News and World Report*, May 26, 1980.
12. Ibid., p. 36.
13. Ibid., p. 517.

14. Ibid.
15. MECS, 1983-84, p. 392.
16. Ibid., p. 788.
17. MECS, 1983-84, p. 392.
18. Ibid., pp. 387-395.
19. Wall Street Journal, October 21, 1983.
20. International Herald Tribune, October 13, 1983.
21. Ha'aretz, January 2, 1984 (citing the Washington Post).
22. New York Times, May 17, 1984.
23. Ibid.
24. International Herald Tribune, May 22, 1984.
25. Kuwait News Agency, May 21, Foreign Broadcast Information Service (Daily Report), May 21, 1984; see also International Herald Tribune, May 22, 1984.
26. Wall Street Journal, June 21, 1984.
27. MECS 1983-84, p. 394.
28. Wall Street Journal, May 22, 1984.
29. New York Times, May 17, 1984; Jerusalem Post (Reuters), May 23, 1984.
30. International Herald Tribune, May 24, 1984.
31. US News and World Report, August 31, 1987.
32. Newsweek, August 3, 1987.
33. US News and World Report, August 31, 1987.
34. International Herald Tribune, June 16, 1987.
35. This chronology is based on US sources. See Caspar W. Weinberger, A Report to the Congress on Security Arrangements in the Persian Gulf, June 15, 1987.
36. Ibid.
37. International Herald Tribune, June 6, 1987.
38. Weinberger, A Report to the Congress.
39. International Herald Tribune, June 20, August 24, 1987; Washington Post, August 29, September 3, 1987.
40. New York Times, October 7, 1987.
41. Weinberger, A Report to the Congress.

42. Washington Post, December 2, 1987.
43. Jacob Goldberg, "Saudi Arabia's Attitude Toward the USSR, 1977-80: Between Saudi Pragmatism and Islamic Conservatism," in Yaacov Ro'i, ed., The USSR and the Muslim World: Issues in Domestic and Foreign Policy (London: George Allen & Unwin, 1984), pp. 261-277.
44. William Quandt, Saudi Arabia in the 1980s (Washington: The Brookings Institution, 1981), p. 70.
45. See for example interview given by Soviet Ambassador to Kuwait Abokov, at the time of Iran's March 1985 offensive. Al-Watan, March 18, 1985. For more recent Soviet warnings to Iran, see statement of chief Soviet delegate to the UN, Alexander M. Belonogov, International Herald Tribune, January 15, 1987.
46. MECS, 1983-84, p. 414.
47. Cordesman, The Gulf and the Search for Strategic Stability, p. 618.
48. MECS, 1986 (forthcoming). See section on Oman.
49. MECS, 1983-84, p. 415.
50. La Vanguardia (Barcelona), July 15, Foreign Broadcast Information Service (Daily Report), July 19, 1985.
51. See explanation by UAE Foreign Ministry Undersecretary

Shaykh Hamdan ibn Zayid, <u>Radio Abu Dhabi</u>, November 15--Foreign Broadcast Information Service (Daily Report), November 15, 1985.
52. <u>The Economist</u>, November 23, 1985.
53. <u>Akbar al-Khalij</u>, June 30--Foreign Broadcast Information Service (Daily Report), July 2, 1985.
54. <u>New York Times</u>, October 22, 1983.
55. <u>MECS</u>, 1983-84, p. 529.
56. <u>Ha'aretz</u>, November 3, 1983.
57. <u>Al-Anba</u>, June 11-12, 1987 (Hatzav--Israel Broadcast Information Service).
58. <u>Al-Ahram</u>, March 14, 21, 1986 (Hatzav).
59. <u>Al-Anba</u>, June 11-12, 1987 (Hatzav).
60. <u>International Herald Tribune</u>, January 25-26, and April 3, 1986.
61. <u>The Economist</u>, December 19, 1987; <u>Jerusalem Post</u>, October 26, 1987; <u>International Herald Tribune</u>, January 4, 1988.
62. <u>Al-Ittihad</u>, April 13, 1987.
63. <u>New York Times</u>, August 20, 1980.
64. Aharon Levran (ed.), <u>The Middle East Military Balance 1986</u>, Jaffee Center for Strategic Studies, Tel Aviv University (Boulder, Colorado: Westview, 1987).
65. <u>Washington Post</u>, November 25, 1984.
66. <u>The Economist</u>, December 12, 1987.
67. <u>Los Angeles Times</u>, December 1, 1985.
68. <u>The Muslim</u> (Islamabad), November 1--Foreign Broadcast Information Service (JPRS), December 15, 1986.
69. <u>Dawn</u> (Karachi), January 17--Foreign Broadcast Information Service (JPRS), March 13, 1987.
70. <u>New York Times</u>, November 1, 1987.
71. <u>Financial Times</u>, November 1, 1983.
72. <u>Al-Qabas</u>, June 29--Foreign Broadcast Information Service (Daily Report), July 2, 1984.
73. <u>Al-Hawadith</u>, July 6, 1984.
74. <u>MECS</u>, 1983-84, pp. 408-409.

Chapter 5

1. "Military Requirements for the Defense of the Middle East" (A Briefing by the Chairman, the Joint Chiefs of Staff for the Deputy Secretary of Defense), JCS 1887/61, November 26, 1952, in Paul Kesaris (ed.), <u>Records of the Joint Chiefs of Staff</u>, Part 2, 1946-53, the Middle East.
2. Interviews (April 1986) by the author: US Department of State, Bureau of Political-Military Affairs; National Security Council; US Department of Defense, Directorate of Plans and Policy (J-5), Joint Chiefs of Staff; Office of the Deputy Undersecretary of Defense for Near East and South Asian Affairs.
3. Cordesman, <u>The Gulf and the Search for Strategic Stability</u>, p. 66.
4. <u>Ibid</u>., p. 944.
5. <u>Ibid</u>., p. 981.
6. Steven J. Rosen, <u>The Strategic Value of Israel</u>, AIPAC Papers on US-Israel Relations.

7.   Alexander Haig, <u>Caveat: Realism, Reagan and Foreign Policy</u> (New York: Macmillan Publishing, 1954), p. 170.

8.   Harry Shaw, "Strategic Dissensus," Foreign Policy, No. 61 (Winter 1985-86), pp. 125-141.

9.   Comment by Edward Luttwak at "Conference on Strategy and Defense in the Eastern Mediterranean," July 4-9, 1986 (Jerusalem, Washington Institute for Near East Policy).

10. John S. Badeau, <u>The American Approach to the Arab World</u> (New York: Harper & Row Publishers, 1968), pp. 123-151.

11. Alexander Bligh, "Towards Israeli-Saudi Coexistence" (Policy Proposal) in <u>The Jerusalem Quarterly</u>, No. 35 (Spring 1985), p. 32.

12. Henry Kissinger, <u>White House Years</u>, pp. 597-631.

13. Stuart E. Eizenstat, "The Next Four Years: The Future of Strategic Cooperation," Address at the Dayan Center, Tel Aviv University, Tel Aviv, Israel, December 28, 1987.

14. <u>International Herald Tribune</u>, October 26, 1987; <u>Jerusalem Post</u>, November 28, 1987.

15. US Congress, Senate Committee on Armed Services, <u>Defense Organization: The Need for Change</u>. Staff Report to the Committee on Armed Services, 99th Congress, First Session, October 16, 1985 (Washington: US Government Printing Office), p. 319.

16. David M. Ransom, Lawrence J. McDonald, W. Nathaniel Howell, "Atlantic Cooperation for Persian Gulf Security," <u>Essays on Strategy</u>, Selections from the 1983 Joint Chiefs of Staff Essay Competition (Washington: National Defense University Press, 1984), p. 91.

17. <u>American-Arab Affairs</u>, No. 20 (Spring 1987), p. 36.

18. Cordesman, <u>The Gulf and the Search for Strategic Stability</u>, p. 978.

19. <u>MECS</u>, 1986 (forthcoming). See section on Oman.

20. Cordesman, <u>The Gulf and the Search for Strategic Stability</u>, p. 978.

21. Maj.Gen.(res.) Abraham Tamir, "Main Considerations of Planning National Security Requirements," Zvi Offer and Maj. Avi Kober (eds.), <u>Quality and Quantity in Military Buildup</u> (Tel Aviv: Ma'arachot--Ministry of Defense Press, 1985, Hebrew), p. 341.

JCSS Publications

JCSS publications present the findings and assessments of the Center's research staff. Each paper represents the work of a single investigator or a team. Such teams may also include research fellows who are not members of the Center's staff. Views expressed in the Center's publications are those of the authors and do not necessarily reflect the views of the Center, its trustees, officers, or other staff members or the organizations and individuals that support its research. Thus the publication of a work by JCSS signifies that it is deemed worthy of public consideration but does not imply endorsement of conclusions or recommendations.

The Jaffee Center for Strategic Studies
Recent Publications in English

1985 Subscription Series

Study no. 1 — Nimrod Novik, *Encounter with Reality: Reagan and the Middle East During the First Term.*

Study no. 2 — Anat Kurz and Ariel Merari, *ASALA: Irrational Terror or Political Tool.*

Study no. 3 — Efraim Karsh, *The Cautious Bear: Soviet Military Engagement in Middle East Wars in the Post 1967 Era.*

Study no. 4 — Shemuel Meir, *Strategic Implications of the New Oil Reality.*

1986 Subscription Series

Study no. 5 — Abraham Ben-Zvi, *The American Approach to Superpower Collaboration in the Middle East, 1973-1986.*

Study no. 6 — Ariel Merari and Shlomi Elad, *The International Dimension of Palestinian Terrorism.*

Study no. 7 — Saul Cohen, *The Geopolitics of Israel's Border Question.*

Study no. 8 — Yehuda Ben-Meir, *National Security Decisionmaking: The Israeli Case.*

1987-88 Subscription Series

Study no. 9 — Asher Arian, Ilan Talmud, Tamar Hermann, *National Security and Public Opinion in Israel.*

Study no. 10 — Aharon Klieman, *Statecraft in the Dark, Israel's Practice of Quiet Diplomacy.*

Study no. 11 — Dore Gold, *America, the Gulf, and Israel: CENTCOM (Central Command) and Emerging U.S. Regional Security Policies in the Middle East.*

Study no. 12 — Ariel Levite, *Offense and Defense in Israeli Military Doctrine.*

JCSS Special Study — Shai Feldman, *U.S. Middle East Policy: The Domestic Setting.*

Books

Shai Feldman, *Israeli Nuclear Deterrence: A Strategy for the 1980s* (New York: Columbia University Press, 1983).

Mark Heller, *A Palestinian State: The Implications for Israel* (Cambridge: Harvard University Press, 1983).

Zvi Lanir, ed., *Israeli Security Planning in the 1980s* (New York: Praeger, 1984).

Aryeh Shalev, *The West Bank: Line of Defense* (New York: Praeger, 1985).

Ariel Merari, ed., *Terrorism and Counter-Terrorism* (Frederick, Md: UPA, 1985).

Nimrod Novik, *The United States and Israel: Domestic Determinants of a Changing US Commitment* (Boulder: Westview, 1986).

Anat Kurz, ed., *Contemporary Trends in World Terrorism* (New York: Praeger, 1987).

Annuals

The Middle East Military Balance.

InTer, A Review of International Terrorism.